MONSTER SQUAT

A Step By Step Guide to a Bigger Squat!

Joe "Ironman" Norman

Edited by GardenWall Publications LLC
http://www.gardenwallpublications.com

MONSTER SQUAT
A Comprehensive Guide to a Bigger Squat!

TABLE OF CONTENTS

Foreword

My name is Lester Estevez and I am a board certified Osteopathic physician and competitive powerlifter. In 1998, I was living in Chicago, attending medical school when I first heard the name Joe Norman. Before I left for college, I was one of the first members of the powerlifting team, Team Jax, based out of Jacksonville, FL. While I was away, I kept in touch with the team and would occasionally hear about all of their various accomplishments. The name Joe Norman kept popping up in team competitions. I remember that Joe was a 198'er that could squat 575 lbs. and deadlift 575 lbs. and according to our coach, "had all of the potential in the world." Being a competitor myself, I thought, "There is no way that this guy can be that good." As fate would dictate, I eventually moved back to Jacksonville, started training with him, and was able to witness the metamorphosis of Joe Norman into Joe "Ironman" Norman.

As Joe and I trained together, we developed a great friendship. To this day I consider him to me one of my very best friends. Joe's personal qualities bubbled to the surface. He has proven to not only be a great training partner, but also to be a true friend. I consider him to be like a brother. His unrelenting pursuit of a "Monster Squat" has fueled his undying dedication to Team Jax and the sport of powerlifting.

He wasn't an overnight success. It has taken years, but I have personally witnessed his development into a champion. His early years in the sport were shaky. He had trouble hitting the "big lifts" in competition. The same lifts he would hit in training. He eventually shook off those "competition demons" and became one of the best pound for pound squatters in the sport. At his age he has broken almost every squat record out there and continues to do so. There's no doubt in my mind that Joe is one of the most gifted squatters to ever compete in the sport of powerlifting.

This book is Joe's way of giving back to the sport. Everything he has learned is detailed in this book. From learning how to squat properly, to competition, it's all here. Joe explains proper squat form, various squatting styles, squatting gear selection, competition squatting, as well as what it take to be in the proper state of mind to perform a big squat. All of these sections are vital to the progression of the squat.

I can remember when we went to the APF Senior Nationals in Detroit, Michigan several years ago and Joe wandered up to the Metal vendor where he purchased a new pair of Metal briefs. At the time, these briefs were new on the market and considered to be very difficult to learn and use. When the team saw him come back with the briefs, we all immediately advised him not to use them, that it was crazy, but as stubborn as he is, he went ahead with his gut instinct and used them. I remember him saying "These briefs are exactly what I've been looking for, I know they will work." I thought that he was doomed to failure for sure. To make a long story short, he used the briefs and ended up squatting his first world record. This is the kind of gifted squatter that I am telling you about. This is my good friend and training partner Joe "Ironman" Norman.

This book is a must read for all of those who want to learn to become a "Monster Squatter". Joe explains how to do it in a simplistic manner with explicit detail. Through his own personal experiences, Joe will help you reach your powerlifting goals. I can still remember that guy that I heard about in 1998 with an impressive 575 lb. squat in the 198 lb. weight class. That same guy has transformed himself into an 1,100+ lb. squatting machine at a body weight of 250 lbs. He has evolved and so will you.

Lester Estevez DO
Doctor of Osteopathic Medicine
Board Certified Family Practice

Preface

What's your bench?

You might think that question is a funny way to start a book about squatting, but you have to understand—that's the first question you get when people find out you are a competitive powerlifter. They don't care about the squat and most don't even know what a deadlift is. On rare occasions, their second question may be "How much can you squat?" When posed with this question, wouldn't it be nice to say "You wouldn't believe me if I told you"? Although a big bench is a great accomplishment and very impressive, there isn't anything that compares to the feeling of euphoria that accompanies a huge squat. There are tons of lifters, competitive powerlifters, and gym rats alike that can push up an impressive bench, but there are few that can put up a monstrous squat.

My intent with this book is to guide you on your quest for a Monster Squat, whether it's for your own personal goal or for competition. This is not one of those "Monster Squat in Six Weeks" kinds of book. Whether your "Monster" is 400, 600, 800, or even 1,000 lbs., the topics I will discuss in this book will help you reach your goal. I will try to make this book useful for beginners, while giving experienced lifters a fresh insight and new ideas about squatting. It will dissect the squat into sections. In the pages of this book I will give you access to everything I've learned over the years that lead to my own success in squatting.

Before we get started, I would like to acknowledge all the members of Team Jax, past and present. Special acknowledgment goes out to Lester Estevez, for providing the team with the proper facility and equipment to train, as well as being one of my constant training partners for years. Also, special acknowledgment goes out to Sylvester Crumbley, for being a steady partner, for all the spotting, as well as advice over the years. I would also like to thank Randy Boynton for all the knowledge passed down. Shouts also need to go out to Toby Irby of Hillbilly Power out of Lake City, FL and the members of Team Sampson of Jacksonville, FL. Last, but certainly not least, I need to give the most acknowledgment to my wife, Kimberly, for putting up with all it takes to be a competitive powerlifter's wife.

I would also like to dedicated this book to the memory Michael Harley Boynton, Jeffrey Bryan Abbott, and all the other powerlifters that have passed from this life the next far too early.

Me squatting 1,003 lbs. @ the APF Single-Ply Nationals

Why Listen to Me?

You may be wondering why you should listen to me. Who am I? What do I know about squatting? What makes me an expert? Those are all good questions. Let me tell you a little about myself. I have no degree of any kind relating to any kind of sport. I don't work in a gym and I have never trained anyone as a personal trainer. In fact, I sit at a desk all day programming computers. I really sound qualified, don't I? Keep reading. It's what I've been doing for the past thirteen years after work and on the weekends that make me the guy you want to listen to.

In 1998, I joined a powerlifting team in Jacksonville, Florida—Team Jax. Team Jax is one of the oldest and most experienced powerlifting teams in the south. The team is currently made up of five dedicated core members and several peripheral members. We apply a modified version of the Westside Barbell training program. We are a competitive team, lifting in raw, single-ply, and multi-ply powerlifting federations. Our members have appeared on the Powerlifting USA's Top 100 lifter lists for years.

Before this, I had been lifting for approximately eight years. Yes, I was a gym rat. I squatted, benched, deadlifted, and did every other exercise you can think of. In fact I even did aerobics. Yes, aerobics. When you stop laughing, I will get on with my story. As I was saying, I was a true gym rat. My squat was pretty impressive. I was backing out and squatting right around 600 lbs. at a body weight of 200 lbs. I was the man! Or at least I thought I was. Funny thing, it was my deadlift that got me noticed. I was deadlifting 550 lbs., when a fellow gym member said that I should try competitive powerlifting. Without getting into too many details, I found Team Jax. On my very first squat training day with the team, my squat went from a 600 lbs. gym squat to a proper 400 lbs. competition squat, instantly.

It was apparent that I didn't know SQUAT about the squat! But I was determined.

My first competition was at age thirty in the United State Powerlifting Federation (USPF), a single-ply federation, in the 198 lb. weight class. I think I squatted 475 lbs. It took almost three more years to get an official 600 lbs. squat. In 2002, the team decided to switch to multi-ply gear, and we started competing in the American Powerlifting Federation (APF). With the advancement in gear and the use of a monolift, my squat excelled quickly. It continued to go up over the years, but it took at least five solid years of training before it really grew.

In the years I have been competitive lifting, I have tried just about every type of single-ply and multi-ply squat suit on the market. I have broken (and still hold) numerous records in multiple federations spanning three weight classes. With little raw lifting, my personal best raw squat is 700 lbs. at 245 lbs. body weight, forty-three years old. My personal best competition squats by weight class are as follows:

Multi-ply gear:

- 831 lbs. @ 198 (198 class), thirty-seven years old

- 1,003 lbs. @ 220 (220 class), forty years old

- 1,014 lbs. @ 242 (242 class), forty-two years old

- 1,105 lbs. @ 249 (275 class), forty-two years old

Single-ply gear:

- 675 lbs. @ 198 (198 class), thirty-eight years old

- 1,010 lbs. @ 256 (275 class), forty-three years old

The numbers speak for themselves. I now know the SQUAT. If you still have any questions you can email me at teamjaxfl@gmail.com or check out the following web links:

About Me:	http://about.me/joeironmannorman
Blog:	http://joeironmannorman.wordpress.com
Twitter:	https://twitter.com/#!/MonsterSquat
YourTube:	http://www.youtube.com/Teamjaxfl
Lifter Profile:	http://joeironmannorman.wordpress.com/about

Enough about me, are you ready to get started?

Squatting is simple:
put the bar on your back,
squat down and
stand back up...

Chapter 1: Squat 101

How to Squat

Jordan (JoJo)
Groff
(710 lbs.)

Squatting is simple, put the bar on your back, squat down and stand back up. Couldn't get any simpler, right? Wrong. The wrong technique (form) for your body type will not only inhibit your full potential, but can also lead to injury.

The way most people squat can be summed up into three techniques: Dive-Bomb, Slow and Steady, and Controlled Blast. I will go into details on these a little later, but first things first—let's discuss the mechanics of the squat.

The squat can be broken down into three sections: setup, squat technique, and recovery. Each has their own parts. Below is a summary of the process, with more details to come.

Setting Up:

- Bar position and grip: Placing the bar on your upper back or lower neck and setting a grip with your hands on the bar.

- Foot placement: Placing your feet in the appropriate position and angle to perform the squat.

- Unracking/backing out: Lifting the weight out of the rack and taking steps backward with the weight to establish your foot position.

Top Three Techniques:

- Dive-Bomb

- Slow and Steady

- Controlled Blast

All techniques have the following common parts:

- Breaking the weight: The initial part of lifting the bar out of the rack.

- Descent: Lowering the bar.

- Getting in the hole/breaking parallel: Reaching the bottom of the squat, at or below parallel.

- Recovery:

   a) Turn the weight around: Changing the direction of the weight when in the hole (the lowest point of the lift).

   b) Drive: Pushing the bar from the lowest position back to a fully upright, standing position.

   c) Sticking points: Any time during the drive when the weight loses momentum; usually occurs when the force applied to pushing the weight switches from one muscle group to another.

Racking the Weight:

- Racking the weight: Placing the bar back into the rack at the end of the squat.

Textbook Definition (Or Something Like That)

Let's pull it all together into a textbook definition on how to squat.

Step up to the bar facing forward. Place your hands on the bar a little wider than shoulder width, and grip the bar. Lower your head under the bar and push your shoulders into the bar, firmly placing the bar on your upper back (bar position). Make sure the bar is centered on your back. For monolift lifters, place your feet under the bar at shoulder width or wider (foot placement). Bend at the knees, keeping your trunk in the most upright position; make sure your head is pulled back with your chest raised. Your lower back should be arched. It is very important to try and keep your back arched throughout the lift. Take a deep breath and hold it. Using your legs, straighten your knees to unrack the bar.

Yury Chakur (505 lbs. for reps)

If you plan on backing the weight out, place your feet close together under the bar. Take a deep breath and bend your knees. Using your legs, straighten your knees to unrack the weight. The weight may be oscillating a little; wait until the weight is steady and you have full control of it before taking any steps backward. Once in control, take a short step back away from the rack, usually with your stronger leg. Follow with the other leg, taking a step back at a slight angle away from your body, placing the foot on the floor toe pointing away from your body. With the first leg, take a step to the side to widen your stance, placing the foot with its toe pointing away from your body (foot placement).

WAIT UNTIL THE BAR STOPS ALL MOVEMENT before attempting to squat. Make sure you have full control of the weight before beginning your descent. With the weight under control, start the descent by pushing your knees out and your hips slightly backward, almost like you were about to sit in a chair (breaking the weight), bending your knees at the same time. Continue to lower the weight until the top surfaces of the legs at the hip joint are even (parallel) or, ideally, lower than the top of your knees (breaking parallel).

Once at the bottom of the descent, reverse the direction of the weight using your legs and your hips (turn the weight around). Continue pushing the weight up (drive) until your body is in a fully upright position and your knees are locked out.

To rack the weight, monolift lifters, your training partners will push the rack arms back into position. Place the bar back into the rack arms, release the bar and step back from the bar. Non-monolift lifters, at the top of the recovery, wait until the bar is motionless, then take steps to get your feet back under your body, one foot at a time. With help from your spotters, step forward to rack the weight, release the bar once it is placed back in the rack, and step back from the bar.

That's pretty much the squat.

The above summary is good and will work for most people, but if you want to achieve a Monster Squat, we need to get into the details, so you will have a better understanding of the variations and be able to decide which variation will help you in your quest.

Setting Up

One of the most important parts of the squat is the set up. When set up properly, you maximize your chances to make the lift. With a poor setup, the weight could become unstable, out of control, feel overwhelming, and ultimately lead to a failed attempt. With the proper setup, you control the weight, which in turn will give you the edge needed to successfully perform the lift. Let's break the setup down into its three parts. They are as follows:

- Bar position and grip: Placing the bar on your upper back or neck and setting a grip with your hands on the bar.

- Foot Placement: Placing your feet in the appropriate position and angle to perform the squat.

- Unracking/backing out: Lifting the weight out of the rack and taking steps backward with the weight and establishing your foot position.

Let's look at these in a little more detail.

Bar Position and Grip

The "bar position" refers to the placement of the bar on your back. "Grip" refers the grip taken on the bar with your hands, as well as the position of the arms and elbows. The three main positions for bar placement are: low (below the trapezius muscles—traps—and just above the shoulder blades), high (on top of traps) or middle (across the middle of the traps, on top of the rear deltoids). Let's go over the benefits and drawbacks of each.

Figure 1:1 - With a low bar, notice the shoulder blades are crunched together with the bar resting at the bottom of the traps.

Low Bar Position

With the older, less supportive gear, lifters often used a low bar position (see Figure 1:1). The belief was that the weight would be closer to a lifter's center of gravity, therefore placing it in a more stable position to squat.

Benefits: The more stable the weight, the easier it is to lift. In addition there is less neck pressure, more surface area contact between your back and the bar, and shorter distance between the bar and the lifter's center of gravity.

Drawbacks: One of the biggest draw backs with this position is that most lifters are not flexible enough in their shoulders and arms to get the bar in the proper position without leaning over a little. This works well for the lighter weights, but as the weights get heavier there is more pressure on the arms and shoulders to hold it in place. What I have witnessed and experienced with this bar position is that most lifters worry more about keeping the bar from sliding down their backs than actually squatting the weight. This ends up putting more pressure on the lower back, especially at the bottom of the lift. That isn't what you want when trying to hit a Monster Squat.

Figure 1:2 - With a high bar the elbows can be placed in a position more under the bar than the other positions. Bar contact with the lifter is at a minimum.

Setup: To set up properly for this bar position, step up to the bar and take a wide grip on the bar. Set the rack or monolift up to line up just below your sternum. You want the bar low in the rack so you will be able to clear the rack when it's placed low on your back. A wide grip will allow you to squeeze your shoulder blades together and allow you to get the bar low on your back without too much stress on your arms and front deltoids, seeing that your arms will be pulled in a position behind your back. For those who are less flexible, it might be necessary to use a false grip. The false grip is when your thumbs are on the same side of the bar as your fingers. With a false grip, you want to make sure you push the bar tight into your back with your palms. It is hard to keep the bar from sliding when using a false grip, so hold tight.

High Bar Position

Let's talk a little about a high bar position (see Figure 1:2).

Benefits: The biggest benefit from this position is that your body can stay in its most upright position throughout the lift. If done correctly, there is no worrying about the bar sliding down your back. Another benefit is that you can help support the bar with your arms and shoulders.

Drawbacks: There are a few drawbacks with this position.

One, it can be hard to keep your head up during the lift with a large amount of weight pushing down on your traps. Second, there is very small surface area contact between you and the bar, making it easier for the bar to

Figure 1:3 - Medium bar with the elbows raised to the sides helping to create a platform across the rear deltoids to support the bar.

become unstable. With the high bar position, you have to make sure you stay upright throughout the lift, especially when you push out of the hole with your legs. When you turn the weight around in the hole and straighten your legs first, this may cause your butt to shoot out and up first, resulting in the bar lining up in front of your knees, "getting out in front" of you. The least that can happen is that you will have to use all of your lower back strength to get the weight back in the proper position to finish the squat. The worst? Maybe injury. The bar can also roll forward higher on to your neck, causing more injury. The neck isn't designed to hold heavy weights.

Setup: To set up for a high bar position, step up to the bar and take a wide grip. A wider grip will be necessary to stabilize the bar. Your grip should be no less than the furthest rings on the bar. Make sure the rack/mono is set high, usually lined up with the top of your sternum. Duck your head under the bar and push your lower neck/upper traps into the bar. Push your body up forcing the bar down onto the top of your traps. Finally, raise your chin tilting your head back as much as is comfortable before unracking the weight.

Medium Bar Position

Last but not least, let's talk about the medium position. If done correctly this position is the most effective (see Figure 1:3).

Benefits: This bar position combines the advantages of the

other two positions. There is just a little less surface area contact than the low bar position, but a lot more than the high bar. With the proper grip, the medium bar position is as stable as the low bar position. With this position, you will be able to take whichever grip you feel most comfortable with. You will also be more capable of keeping your body in an upright position throughout the lift, as well as keeping your head up.

Drawbacks: I really can't think of any drawbacks for this position.

Setup: When setting up for this position, you want to have the rack/mono lined up roughly vertically centered with your sternum. Take a comfortable grip on the bar. A good grip is just a little wider than shoulder width. Duck your head under the bar and push your middle traps into the bar. Push your body up until the bar settles on the bottom of your lower traps and lines up with the top of your rear deltoids. If done correctly, you will feel the bar settle into place.

Bar Position Summary

To summarize, a low bar puts the bar closest to your center of gravity with the maximum amount of bar contact, while also creating stability throughout the lift, but pulling the arms and shoulders behind your back, making it hard to hold the bar in place without leaning forward. The high bar gives you the least amount of bar contact, but allows you to stay in the most upright position. If you lean over at any time on the recovery, there is a high probability you will miss the lift. With a medium bar, there is enough bar contact to help support the bar, making it easier to hold, as well as stabilizing it throughout the lift.

Grip

Now that you know the basics of bar position, let's talk a little more about your grip and arm position. Your grip should be what is most comfortable to you and will vary according to the bar position you choose. However, certain grips work best with each bar position.

When using a high bar, it is best to take a wide grip with your elbows under the bar, almost like you were going to shoulder press the bar. This stabilizes the bar. Also, with your elbows under the bar, you will be able to push the bar up, relieving pressure on your neck.

The best grip for a low bar is to pinch the shoulder blades together and try to keep your arms bent at the elbows at roughly 90 to 110 degrees, with the elbows behind the bar. If at all possible, try to hold the bar with a full grip, thumbs wrapped around the bar. If you aren't flexible enough, you may want to use the false grip, but remember, use your palm to push the bar tight into your back for support.

As for the medium bar, you can grip the bar in pretty much any position you want. Whichever grip you decide to use, you need to try and make a platform with your shoulders and arms for the bar to rest on. This can be accomplished by lifting your elbows up to the sides, then rotating them back. The bar should be resting across your rear delts and lower traps. This can be done with both a wide and a narrow grip.

My 700 lb. raw personal record

Play around with your grip—you will see which one will suit you best. Start out with the ones mentioned here and try some variations of each until you find the one that works. The most important thing to remember is that for a max lift you must be as comfortable as possible.

Foot Placement

Once you have mastered the bar position of your choice, the next thing you have to worry about is your feet. Proper foot placement is essential to a successful squat. Where you place your feet for optimum performance is based on two key factors: your leg strength and flexibility. Let's go over a few positions that most lifters use.

Where you decide to place your feet is going to be based on your flexibility and leg strength. For example, if your hip flexors aren't very flexible and you have strong quadriceps (quads), then a closer stance will work. The more flexible you are in your hips, the more a wider stance will work.

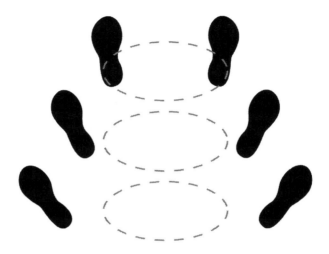

There are a few things to consider when deciding what stance to use. Generally, the wider the stance, the more the hips, glutes, and hamstrings are used to push the weight. The closer the stance, the more involved the quads are. One of the biggest things to consider is comfort—you want to pick a stance that is comfortable to you. Ideally, you want a stance that lets you squat down below parallel, with your back in the most upright position, arched at the base, chest up, shoulders back, all while keeping your knees from floating out over your toes, the whole time being comfortable. Sounds impossible? Not really. It's won't happen overnight. It will take some experimenting on your part to find the stance that works best for you. Experiment with stance width and toe positions using slight variation of each until you find the one that is best.

Figure 1:4 - Common foot placement

Look at figure 1:4. The dotted line represents your torso and of course the black foot shapes represent your feet. At the top, you will see that the feet are placed straight down under the body, hip-width apart, toes pointing out very slightly. This is the common close stance. As you look down at the image, you will notice that as the feet get farther apart the toes are being pointed out more each time. By pointing your toes out, this will allow your hips to open up more in the hole.

Here's a good exercise that will help you find a good starting point. Take a box that is roughly equal to the height of your knees from the floor. If you are new to squatting below parallel, start with an ordinary chair instead of a box. Place a broomstick or just a bar on your back using the bar position you decided to go with. Now, stand in front of the box with your feet placed, as shown in Figure 1:4 for a close stance. You want to be at least a foot in front of the box. With your lower back arched, head and chest up, and shoulders back, push your butt back and squat down to the box. Try to keep your knees from floating out in front of your toes on the way down. Once you reach the box stand back up. Squat down a few more times, changing your toe position each time.

Repeat this exercise with the other two stances shown in Figure 1:4. As your stance gets wider, you will want to push your knees out as you descend. This can be accomplished by spreading your legs. As you try these exercises, you want to take note of the one that meets all the criteria mentioned before. You want to start with the stance that came closest and work from there. When you are finished experimenting, try it with some light weight and compare the results. The results may vary, but you will be able to figure out which stance is the best for you.

Unracking/Backing Out

Now that you have your bar position and foot placement mastered, it's time to unrack the weight. Unracking the weight may be a small part of the lift, but it is not any less important than the rest. If you unrack the weight wrong it could feel like you have the weight of the world on your back, but when done correctly, the weight will feel light and you will be in control. There's nothing like the feeling you get when unracking a heavy weight, with the bar planted firmly on your back, the weight pushing down on you, all while staying in control.

Before you unrack the weight you want to make sure the rack is set to the appropriate height. For those who plan on using a monolift, start with just the bar at a height around mid-sternum. Duck under the bar to get it into the bar position you plan on using. Place your feet into your desired position by bending your knees as much as needed. Make sure to get your body in the most upright position. Using your legs, straighten your knees out to raise the bar out of the monolift arms. Check the distance between the bar and the lift's arms. You want that distance to be only a few inches. If the bar is any more than six inches from the arms, raise the monolift. Another thing to watch out for when using a monolift is that the bar comes straight up off the arms. You don't want the bar to run up the front of the arms as you unrack it. This means you are standing too far forward under the lift, so pull both feet back. If the bar ends up out of the arms far enough to squat without having to pull the lever on the lift, then you are standing too far back from the lift—place your feet further forward.

For those who plan on backing out the weight, you want to start by getting the bar into the desired position on your back. You want to have the rack set to a height that allows you to stand with both feet close together under the bar, knees slightly bent. With your back in the proper position, stand up the same as described above, by straightening your knees. Make sure the bar comes straight up out of the rack, clearing it by only a few inches.

There are a few things to keep in mind when unracking the weight. As the weight gets heavier you need to keep an eye on the amount the bar bends. When you get up to the monster weight, the bar will be bending, so you might have to lower the lift/rack to compensate. Also take note, if you have the arms of the monolift or the rack set to a wide position, you may not notice the bend until you unrack the weight. Speaking about rack width, if you plan on backing the weight out of a wide rack, take care not to hit the racks with the weights as you step backward.

So far, you have the bar positioned, your feet planted, and the rack set to the appropriate height. It's time to unrack the weight. There are two methods used most often. The first is to power the weight out. To do this, take a deep breath, then push up hard and explosively with your legs. The weight will come out of the rack with force and speed. The benefits are that you don't feel the force of the weight much until you are already standing with it. The drawback is that the weight can become unstable. The bar will tend to bend and recoil a little, making it harder to control. The second method is to control the weight out of the rack. To do this, take a deep breath and slowly push your body up into the weight, use your legs and hips to steadily push the weight up out of the rack. You will feel the weight more this way and it will come up slower, but you will maintain control over it at all times. Either method will work fine, just remember the most important thing: don't attempt to squat until the weight stops all motion. If you are using a monolift, you are ready to squat. For those who are backing out the weight, you are almost ready.

When backing weight out, you want to take small steps. There is no reason to walk back far away from the rack. You only need to be far enough back not to hit the rack during the lift. As I mentioned earlier, take a deep breath and unrack the weight with your feet close together directly under the bar. You may want to have one foot placed a little forward, as this can make it easier to take a step backwards. While holding your breath, take a step back. Some lifters like to take a step at an angle away from the center of their body, so all they have to do is take another angled step with the other foot and they will be step up ready to squat. I call this the two-step method. When you step back at an angle, if you don't shift the weight appropriately to the non-moving foot, you put yourself at risk of

Sylvester (Sly) Crumbley (970 lbs.)

injury. The second step of this method makes it hard to control the weight due to the angle your leg will be at from the initial step. If you plan on using this method, take it slow and make sure the weight stops all motion before taking each step.

Another back-out method is what I like to call the step, step, and side step. Take your breath as before, and take a step directly back away from the rack. Follow with the other leg. Once both feet are together, there are two options. One, take one step to the side as far as you need to get into position. Two, take a side step with one foot then one more with the other to get into position. If you elect to use the first, you won't be centered with the rack, but that doesn't really matter, the rack is irrelevant during the rest of the squat.

Either method mentioned above will most likely take one whole breath to perform, once settled, you will want to take another before starting your descent. You are now setup and ready to squat.

Technique

So, now that you mastered the setup, what's next? Squat down and stand up, right? Not so fast. You need to decide on a technique. There are so many different techniques you can use to lower the weight, with tons of variations on each, so I have decided to discuss the top three according to my opinion.

Now, I'm sure you are wondering how I came to pick these three. The three I'm going to discuss are the most common I've seen competitive powerlifters use. I can tell you that I haven't seen anyone who squats super heavy weight not use at least one of these, or a slight variation of one.

The three most common techniques are as follows:

- Dive-Bomb

- One Motion

- Controlled Blast

Every technique has the following common parts:

- Breaking the weight: The initiation of the squat.

- Descent: Lowering the weight.

- In the hole/breaking parallel: The bottom of the squat, at or below parallel.

- Recovery:

    a) Turn the weight around: Change the direction of the weight when in the hole (at the bottom of the lift).

    b) Drive: Pushing the weight from the squat position back to an upright position.

    c) Sticking Points: Any time during the drive when the weight stops momentum, usually occurs when the force applied to pushing the weight switches from one muscle group to another.

The next step is to figure out which technique will work best for you.

Dive-Bomb

The Dive-Bomb technique is very simple. This technique is almost a full free-fall of the weight.

1. Breaking the weight: To break the weight with this technique, start by pushing your butt back and relaxing the muscles in your legs.

2. Descent: The descent is pretty easy—allow the weight to come down fast. Keep the weight under control, but bring it down fast.

3. In the hole/breaking parallel: When you reach the hole, the speed of the weight will help you break parallel.

4. Turn the weight around: Keeping your back tight, use your glutes and hamstrings to rebound the weight out of the hole.

5. Drive: The speed of the bar coming up from the rebound will help your legs drive the weight back up.

6. Sticking points: The speed of the weight should help you through most sticking points.

This technique relies on speed and the rebound effect of your body to turn the weight around at the bottom, almost like it bounces back. It is a good technique for lifters with limited flexibility due to the fact that the speed of the weight will help them break parallel. Personally, I like to use this when warming up. It's a good way to stretch your muscles.

Benefits from this technique are as mentioned earlier, namely that it helps you break parallel. You don't spend a lot of energy lowering the weight, which leaves your body in a good condition to push the weight back up. When your body's natural reflexes kick in at the bottom, the force needed to turn the weight's direction back around is limited, leaving more energy for your body to use in the recovery.

There are drawbacks with this technique. When the weights get really heavy and are moving fast, your body will have a harder time changing the momentum of the weight. Another drawback is lack of control. You can control the weight on the way down as much as possible, but once your reflexes kick in at the bottom and turn it around, there is a possibility of losing control. An example you will see most often is a lifter's butt coming up first, causing the weight to get pushed out in front of their body. This is usually caused by a weak lower back. The back is strong enough to hold the weight on the way down, but not strong enough to stay erect when it's time to stop and turn the weight around.

There are a few key things to watch out for. When done properly the weight will tend to recoil from the quick change in direction, so you will want to practice this with the lighter

Yury (860 lbs.)

weight and work up to the heavy weight. What I mean by recoil is the bar will change direction before the weights do, causing the bar to bend. Then, the weights will change direction and shoot up with some force, causing them to come up faster than the bar for a split second, essentially bouncing up and down on each side. The recoil usually happens on the way up right after you come out of the hole, so be ready. Tighten your lower back, push your belly into your belt, and hang on. Make sure the weight doesn't throw you forward.

One Motion

This technique is just like it sounds. Bring the weight down with one constant speed and push it back up at the same speed.

    1. Breaking the weight: You want to break the weight

in the same way as the Dive-Bomb: push you butt back and start the descent.

2. Descent: On the descent you will bring the bar down at a steady speed. The speed is up to you, but you want to move it at a good pace. The whole point is to bring it down in full control.

3. In the hole/breaking parallel: Once in the hole, you will have to judge when you make parallel, the speed of the weight won't be fast enough to help you break parallel.

4. Turn the weight around: You will want to try and turn the weight around at the same speed as the descent. Turn the weight around by pushing your hips forward, while keeping your back tight. It is important not to bend over at the waist and let your butt come up first.

5. Recovery: Try to bring the weight back up at the same speed or faster than your descent speed. When done properly, the squat from top to bottom and back to top should look as though it was one motion.

6. Drive: You will have to push with your legs and thrust your hips forward pretty hard; there will be little rebound bar speed to help.

7. Sticking points: You will also have to deal with any sticking points the same way: push your knees out and drive your hips through the bar

The One Motion technique is the best way to stay in control of the weight at all times. That is the biggest benefit. Maintaining control over the weight makes it hard for something to go wrong. If something does go wrong, you should be able to compensate in time to fix it.

The drawback to this technique is that you will feel the brunt of the weight throughout the whole movement. Also, you will have to hold the weight for a longer time. You will need to build up some endurance for this technique to be effective. Another drawback is the difficulty of breaking parallel. The bar won't be moving fast enough to force you down, so you will have to judge parallel for yourself.

Since you will have total control over the bar at all times during the lift, there isn't much to watch out for. All you will have to train for is the strength and endurance. You want to train your muscles to be able to hold the weight for an extended period of time while holding a deep breath. Make sure you "stay tight" throughout the lift.

Controlled Blast

With this technique you will use a slow, steady, controlled descent and a fast recovery.

1. Breaking the weight: Start this technique the same as the others—by pushing your butt back.

2. Descent: Bring the weight down at one steady speed. Make sure you have total control of the weight at all times.

3. In the hole/breaking parallel: Once you break parallel, use your hips and legs to exert as much force as possible—"explode"—to change the weights direction and start the recovery.

4. Recovery: You will want to push your hips forward and try to force your feet through the floor.

5. Turn the weight around: Think of it as though you were trying to jump off the floor. All this should happen in a split second. The point is to get the bar moving in the opposite direction with as much speed as possible.

6. Drive: The force you use to explode the weight will help with the drive on the way up. Try your best to keep applying as much force as possible after the initial burst.

7. Sticking points: If you can keep the bar moving up with speed, it will be easier when hitting any sticking points on the way up.

The benefits for this technique are the same for the descent as the One Motion technique and the same for the recover from the Dive-Bomb. To recap, you will have full control over the bar on the descent, making it less likely for an error to occur, and if you "explode" properly out of the hole you will have the benefit of bar speed on the way up.

The drawbacks for this technique are similar to the others as well. You will still have to hold the weight for a longer period of time on the descent, as well as pay more attention to breaking parallel. On the way up, the bar should be moving relatively fast, so there could be a little loss of control.

This is a very effective technique for all types of lifters, but it takes a lot of practice. You will have to train your muscles to fire at the appropriate time. Timing is everything. Practice this technique on every weight, even when using just the bar.

You want your muscles to remember when they are supposed fire. Practice until it becomes second nature for them.

There are some issues to watch out for. You will be exerting a lot of force out of the hole, so make sure your butt doesn't come up first. Keep your head up, chest out, and lower back tight. Push your belly into your belt, and then explode. Watch out for recoil as well. If you explode with a lot of force, the bar can tend to recoil.

Whichever technique you decide to go with, try to bring the bar down in a straight line. Remember the exercise from the foot stance section? Try that exercise again with a little variation. Stand up with the bar and get into your stance. Now, have a training partner hold a broomstick or a two-by-four board straight up from the floor directly in front of the bar. Now squat. Try to keep the bar the same distance away from the stick all the way down and back up. To start you will need to push you butt back as though you were trying to sit in a chair. Also, as you lower the weight, try to keep your knees from floating out over your toes. You can accomplish this by pushing your knees out and spreading your groin. When your knees end up over your toes, most of the force needed to recover the weight has to be generated from your quads, taking your hips out of the lift. The ideal position for your legs throughout the squat is to have your shin perpendicular with the floor, ankle at approximately a 90 degree angle. This takes pressure off the knee joint and utilizes more of your thigh and hip muscles for the lift. Practice this exercise with slight variations to your stance until you master it.

Here are a few helpful pointers to help you master your technique:

- First, when you break the weight, start by forcing your butt back and bending at your hips. This immediately forces your hips to help your back support the weight.

- Maintain control of the bar as much as possible. Having control of the bar will help you recover from most things that can go wrong during the lift.

- Push you knees out laterally. You want your shins to be perpendicular to the floor. Just spread your knees out on the way down.

- Keep your back arched and in the most upright position throughout the lift. Keeping your head up and chest out will help keep your back in position.

- "Stay tight." Keep your breath held, push your belly into your belt, shoulders and arms firmly gripping the bar, head up, chest out; every muscle that isn't involved in moving the weight should be used to support and control the weight.

- If your toes or heels come up at all during the lift, you need to adjust your stance. First try pointing your toes in or out before adjusting the width of your stance. I actually point my right toe out more than my left. There is no rule about being symmetrical, just do what works for you.

- If your knees push in when you start to recover the weight, you are probably standing too wide. Bring your stance in until it stops.

- Did you have to lean over at the bottom to break parallel? Yes. You will need to play around with you stance. The most common cause of this is inflexible hip flexors. Try pointing your toes out a little. The more you point out your toes, the easier it is for your hips to open up. The reverse is also true—if you are finding it too easy to break parallel you can point your toes forward to allow your hips to lock up at the bottom, which forces the weight to push you down.

- Trust your partners. Listen to what they say. They will be able to notice things that you can't while squatting. Learn to take constructive criticism.

Racking the Weight

Now that you've found the technique that's going to give you that Monster Squat, there's only one more topic to talk about and you will be ready to squat: racking the weight. There really isn't much to say about this, but it's important nonetheless.

As a monolift lifter, you won't have too much to worry about. Your partner will be pushing the arms back into place once you complete the lift. The main thing to do is to wait for the arms to be locked into place before placing the bar back into them. Sometimes the weight will slide down your back, especially during a heavy lift. You may need your partners to lift up on each side of the bar to guide it into the arms. Make sure the weight is in the arms before releasing it. Also don't turn your head to either side to check if you are in the arms. This isn't good for your neck and can lead to injury. Your partners should make sure you are in.

For those who are backing the weight out of a rack, make sure the bar is motionless at the top of the lift, and then bring your feet together before attempting to walk back toward the racks. Don't take a step toward the rack with your legs spread apart, as you will probably not clear the rack and you will be putting your legs at an odd angle to support the weight. It never hurts to have a training partner on each side help support the weight as you walk it back in. Once your feet are together, step approach the rack until the bar is in. Don't take one step and lean forward to re-rack the weight. You will see lifters do this all the time. This is lazy and dangerous. If you miss the rack, the weight will be out in front of you and you risk hurting your back and neck. Same thing applies as above—don't turn your head.

Summary

Now that you know all you need to know about the mechanics of the squat, you need to experiment. Try different bar positions, grips. Try different stances. Try all three techniques. When you experiment, make sure the weight is fairly light, something you can handle in case something goes wrong. Also, have your spotters/training partners keep their eyes on you for some constructive criticism. Like I said earlier, they will see things you don't. When you find what works for you, practice, practice, practice. Practice on every set, even the warm-up sets. Get your body used to your setup and technique until it becomes second nature. This will build you a good base to work with. Once you have decided on what kind of lifting gear you will use, you may have to alter pieces of this base, but for the most part, it will work out fine. We will go over gear in Chapter 3. For now, stay raw and start squatting.

Treat the heavy weights
like they're light and
the light weight
like they're heavy.

Chapter 2: Training

The Basics

**Lester Estevez
(860 lbs.)**

Learn How to Get Strong

We can get straight into the exercises, but first, we need to talk about you. Your body isn't like everyone else's. Training methods that work for me or for someone else may not work for you. It is up to you to figure out which work best for you.

A friend of mine recently told me the hardest part of strength training is to "learn how to get strong." You can read and read all the over the internet about strength training, different programs, exercises and methods. With so many exercises, routines and methods, what should you do? I can't tell you. That one you will have to figure out for yourself. What I can tell you is what you will need to learn:

- Your body

- Your limits

- Your strengths

- Your weaknesses

- When to push yourself

- When to take it easy

All of these are easy to figure out. All you have to do is pay attention to what you are doing. It's a good idea to keep a log. Write down your sets, reps, weights, and how you felt for every workout. Also, write down how you felt the days after each workout, during the recovery period. This will give you good

insight into what exercises are working best for you. If you can, video record each workout; this way you can see yourself in action. You will be able to see what mistakes you made, as well as the things you did right. Videos are the best way to work on your form. Listen to your training partners' advice, because your partners will see things you won't. Above all, "Train Smart!" Don't let you ego get in the way. If you are having a bad day, stop. Don't let your ego push you to the point where you get hurt.

Sly (800 lbs.)

So, how do you start? We'll get into details later in this chapter when we discuss different programs. But, before we get into any exercises and programs, let's go over strength training in general and how it relates to the quest for a Monster Squat.

Training Your Body and Mind

To squat heavy weight, it's not all about having strong muscles. Don't get me wrong, you will need strong muscles, but that alone isn't going to cut it when you get under the monster weights. Your mind has to be ready as well. Not just your mind, like your state of mind and thoughts, but your mind physically, as in brain and spinal cord. If you try to get under a monstrous amount of weight without being ready for it, you are setting yourself up for disaster and possible injury.

Like I said earlier, when it comes to strength training, there are so many methods, programs, opinions, etc... Whatever method you follow, and however you decide to train, there are a few things you will need to know if you plan on squatting big. Those things are muscle memory and your central nervous system (CNS).

Muscle Memory

Let's start with muscle memory. Muscle memory can be defined in two ways: 1) as it pertains to learning new motor skills or 2)as it is used as slang when pertaining to strength training. Funny enough, the only one you need to be worried about right now is how it pertains to learning motor skills.

Muscle Memory:

Muscle memory has been used synonymously with motor learning, which is a form of procedural memory that involves consolidating a specific motor task into memory through repetition. When a movement is repeated over time, a long-term muscle memory is created for that task, eventually allowing it to be performed without conscious effort. This process decreases the need for attention and creates maximum efficiency within the motor and memory systems. (From Wikipedia, the free encyclopedia, http://en.wikipedia.org/wiki/Muscle_memory)

One of the best examples of muscle memory at work is a baby learning how to walk. The first steps a baby takes are very awkward and unstable, but the more the baby walks, the better they get at walking. Each time the baby walks, the CNS is strengthening and adding connections made between the muscles involved and the brain, until walking becomes "second nature" and they walk without even thinking about it. This is the baby's brain mapping out what it takes to walk, the coordinated effort of all the muscles involved, knowing when and at what time each needs to contract or relax to do its part. This mental "blueprint" is now saved and can be easily called upon for the rest of the baby's life to perform the action of walking.

How does this pertain to squatting? Think about this: when squatting, connections are made between the muscles involved and your brain, enabling your muscles to perform the squat. The more you squat, the stronger those connections get. The more you squat using the same technique, the stronger the connections get with that technique. See where I'm going here? When you perform the same actions (technique) over and over you are creating a mental blueprint on how to squat. In weightlifting lingo, this is called your "form." Throughout the squat there is a sequence of movements, of muscles contracting and relaxing. To squat monster weight, all your muscles will need to know exactly when and what they need to do without you having to think about it.

I'm not sure who came up with this one, but it's a good rule to train by: "Treat the heavy weights like they're light and the light weights like they're heavy." Use the same form on every set, from warm-up to max-rep set. Mastering your form will build and strengthen the connections between your brain and muscles. When your brain can control these movements without thinking about it just by calling upon your "squat blueprint," all you have to worry about is gaining the strength to handle the heavy weights. If you are planning on squatting heavy, you need this blueprint so deeply etched in your brain that squatting becomes like walking to you.

Central Nervous System (CNS)

Have you ever gotten under a heavy weight, unracked it, and out of nowhere your body started to shake? It may have been a weight you have already squatted in the past but haven't attempted in a long time. The "shakes" don't necessarily mean you aren't strong enough to lift the weight, but in fact your body isn't ready to handle it. This would be your CNS telling your body that it isn't ready for the weight. If you are planning on accomplishing a Monster Squat you will need to learn how to get your body and—more importantly—your CNS ready for the weight.

Your CNS consists of your brain and spinal cord. Its main function, to put it simply, is to control all of the physical activity of your body. It sends signals through your peripheral nervous system to your muscles. These pathways or connections are made every time your body experiences something new. Here are the things to know about your CNS when training for a heavy squat:

First, the more stress you put on your body, the more your CNS will adapt to handle that stress. When you put more stress on your muscles than they can handle, your CNS will respond by causing muscle growth to handle that stress. What does this mean when squatting? Well, exactly what it states. You need to squat heavy to be able to squat heavy. Handling medium and light weight for reps just isn't going to be enough. You need to squat heavy weights, overload your muscles with weight, and cause your CNS to make your muscles grow.

Be careful though. You want to work up to these overload weights. Your CNS also has a defense mechanism, which will "shut your body down." This is a protective mechanism that is built into everyone and can be a hassle when training for a heavy squat. Your brain will try to protect your body from hurting itself. When exposed to too much stress too fast, it will stop your muscles from exerting too great a force, which may hurt them. It can be avoided by taking gradual weight increases each week until you obtain your goal. With this gradual progression of weight, your brain will become accustomed to the heavy loads, and each week you will be able to push your body a little harder.

The other thing you can do to force your CNS to cause strength gains is to change things up. Change the exercises and the intensity of your workouts regularly. This will help you avoid the dreaded weight training plateau. This is when you stop progressing. If you want to squat the monster weight, you need to avoid or break through these plateaus. When you perform the same exercise every week, for a long period of time, your body becomes accustomed to it and it will be hard to make progress.

Plateaus and Overtraining

The biggest cause of a plateau is overtraining. Overtraining is like a cold—it kind of sneaks up on you. One minute you are feeling good, the next you kind of feel a little cold coming on. If you ignore it, out of nowhere you will have a full blown cold.

Symptoms of overtraining are pretty easy to see. First, you stop making gains each week. Sometimes the weights you are lifting actually regress. Second, it takes longer to recover from each workout. Third, you start feeling like you don't even want to train. You will find yourself fatigued and lacking motivation. Strength regression and loss of motivation seem to be the worst of these symptoms.

Your goal is to avoid overtraining. When you squat heavy, you are putting an extreme amount of stress on your whole body, especially your back and legs. You need adequate time for these muscles to recover. Avoid putting repeated stress on these muscles until they have time to recuperate. You want to avoid other whole-body exercise like deadlifting.

- Change things up. Change the exercise every one to two weeks. Most of the squat exercises I will mention later work different parts of the squat and different areas of your muscles. Working different parts of the muscles each week will give the parts not being worked more time to recover.

- Change your intensity. Drop the weights and do more reps. By using lighter weights and upping the reps, you will be moving approximately the same volume of weight per workout, but it will be less stressful and easier to recover from.

- Get more rest. Take longer rest periods between sets. Space your workouts an extra day apart. Go to bed early. There are hundreds of ways to rest—think of a few yourself and use them.

If you find yourself still on a plateau, then take a week off. Yes, take a week off from all lifting. Give your body some extra time to recover. Don't worry, you won't lose any gains you've made. Time off from lifting will help you physically, and, if you are like any other lifter I know, after a week you will want to get back in the gym so bad, it will spark your motivation. When you get back into the gym your muscles will remember the weight (muscle memory slang).

Let's do a quick summary of this section. To squat heavy weights you want to work on your form until it becomes second nature to you. You should overload your body with the appropriate stress to force strength gains. Also, you must avoid overtraining.

Strength Training for a Monster Squat

So how do we train for a Monster Squat? I'll break it down for you. Here's a check list:

- Exercise selection
- Frequency of training
- Sets and Reps
- Recovery

What Exercises Do You Need?

This is a simple one. Squat, squat and squat. To squat heavy, you need to get your body used to handling heavy weights. There are all kinds of squat exercises that can be used to help you accomplish this as well as some that will help you train specific parts of the traditional squat. To name a few, there are Box Squats, Chain Squats, Band Squats, Reverse Band Squats, Safety Bar Squats, Manta Ray Squats, Cambered Bar Squats, Front Squats, Good Mornings and Zercher Squats. Each of these exercises has a specific purpose. Some are to help your lower back get stronger, some help your technique, and some help you get accustomed to handling heavy weights.

Me (655 lbs. bar + 360 lbs. chains)

Box Squats are a great exercise to work on your form, as well as to develop the "blasting out of the hole" strength. Chain Squats and Reverse Band Squats are the perfect exercise to overload the weight at the top of the squat. They also help develop transition speed during the recovery part of the squat. Safety, Manta Ray, Cambered, Good Mornings and Front Squats help to build your lower back strength. Zercher squats help build up leg strength. Band squats are great for overall strength.

I suppose you want to know how to choose which ones to use. It's best to perform these exercises in a rotation, but if you need to concentrate on a weakness, you may want to use one or two of them more often. Once you figure out your weakness, you will be able to put a program together that will target those weaknesses and make you stronger. I will give you some example programs later in the chapter that you can choose or use as a template for your own training.

How Often Should You Squat?

Most people train the squat once a week. This is good and sufficient for most lifters, but if you want to squat the monster weights, you need to squat twice a week. If you have read anything about powerlifting, you have probably heard something about Max Effort and Dynamic Effort, from Louie Simmons of Westside Barbell. For years, Louie's methods for strength training have been used by the powerlifting community with great success.

Yury (505 lbs.)

Max Effort, simply put, is lifting up to a maximum 1 rep with heavy weight. Dynamic Effort is lifting for speed with a non-maximum weight. I like to put this in simpler terms, heavy day and light day. You should incorporate these three days in your training week. Try to space them apart by at least two days. If you perform your heavy day on Monday, then you want your light day on Thursday. You want enough time between days to recover from each.

The effort, sets, and reps involved for each day are very different, but you will be lifting close to the same amount of weight in volume. Here is an example:

	Heavy Day MAX 955 lbs. 1 Rep	Light Day Approx. 40% * 955 lbs. 6 sets x 2 reps
	135 x 3	135 x 3
	235 x 3	235 x 3
	325 x 3	325 x 3
	415 x 1	365 x 2
	505 x 1	365 x 2
	595 x 1	365 x 2
	685 x 1	365 x 2
	775 x 1	365 x 2
	865 x 1	365 x 2
	955 x 1	
Total Weight Moved:	6,880 lbs.	6,465 lbs.

When you look at the example above, you can see that the total volume (weight moved) are close. The difference is in how you will move the weight. On the heavy day, depending on how many training partners you have, the time between sets will be anywhere from 10-15 minutes. Each rep will be performed at normal speed and technique, roughly 5-10 seconds. To sum it up, you will be exerting a great deal of force and energy every 10-15 minutes for 5-10 seconds. This is when your body will gain most of its strength.

On the light day, it's all about speed. What I mean by speed is the sets and reps need to be performed fast. One minute between each working set (365 in the above example) of three reps. You want to keep your form as strict as possible and perform all three reps in the same amount of time it takes to do a heavy squat, 5-10 seconds. You will use about 40-50% of your max single. This is when you want to work on your form. This is the day when you will be building your "squatting blueprint," so make sure every rep is completed in form.

Sets and Reps

On your heavy days, you want to have at least three or four warm-up sets with 3-5 reps each and 7-8 heavy sets with 1-3 reps each. For you older lifters, like me, you might want to take a few more warm-up sets. There is a saying in strength training, "heavy threes." This is doing sets with three reps going up in weight until you can't do a set of three with a weight. This is good for beginners trying to build a base and even good to incorporate once in a while for you experienced lifters. However, when you are planning on squatting huge weights, it's my opinion that you need to get your body used to handling those weights. By performing single rep sets, you will be able to do more sets with heavier weights in the same workout.

Here's another thing to think about for your heavy days. The stronger you are, the more volume you will perform during each workout; the weaker you are, the less volume. Let's say your current max is 550 lbs. and you want to squat up to 90% of your max. Look at the two workouts below:

	Plate Jumps	Plate/Quarter Jumps
	135 x 3	135 x 3
	195 x 3	195 x 3
	235 x 3	235 x 3
	325 x 1 (60%)	285 x 1
	415 x 1	325 x 1 (60%)
	505 x 1	375 x 1
		415 x 1
		465 x 1
		505 x 1
Total Weight Moved (TWM):	**2,940 lbs.**	**4,065 lbs.**

The first workout represents taking plate jumps (90 lbs.) between sets and the second plate/quarter (90 lbs. and 50 lbs. alternating) jumps between sets. Note the differences. On the first workout, there are three sets performed at or above the 60% of the 550 max with total (TWM) of 2,940 lbs. While on the second workout, five sets at or above the 60% of the max with TWM of 4,065 lbs. As you can see, the max weight for each workout was the same but it is clear that second workout will put more stress on your body.

Taking the appropriate jumps is a good thing to keep in mind when planning your workouts. If your goal for a workout is to squat a max weight, you may want to take larger jumps. This allows you to save energy for your max set by limiting the number of sets. If you want to get a lot of volume in a workout, take smaller jumps or perform more rep sets. You can use these theories for planning your workouts even based on how you feel that day. If you are feeling fatigued, but still want to hit a heavy weight, do bigger jumps, less sets. If you are feeling great and need extra volume to promote strength growth, do more sets, more reps, and smaller jumps. Get the picture?

I would suggest one thing: write it down. Keep track of the exercise, sets and reps and weights you do, so the next time you come back to the same exercise, you can plan your workout accordingly to gauge your progress.

Recovery

Recovery times vary from lifter to lifter, but the rule of thumb in any kind of weight training is that the muscles need an average of forty-eight hours to recover, and the larger the muscles the longer the recovery. Being that your legs are one of the largest muscle groups in your body, it may take a little longer to recover.

It's not just your legs that need to recover. Squatting is considered a "whole body" exercise. The stress put on your body isn't just localized to the legs. The lower back is highly taxed. The shoulders and arms have to support the weight. The abs and obliques are involved in stabilizing the weight. Almost every muscle in your body has a part in squatting. When planning your workouts, take this into consideration.

Let's say you train heavy bench and shoulders on Monday. You want to wait until the end of the week before trying to squat heavy. If you are anything like most powerlifters, your shoulders and arms will probably feel sore until Wednesday, not to mention your back in some cases. Now this book isn't on benching, but believe it or not your back, in particular your Latissimus dorsi muscles (lats), play a role in benching, especially if you bench with a wide grip. The lower back also plays a part, especially if you bench with a high arch in your back. It's not uncommon for your back to feel sore for a few days after benching. You want most of the soreness to be gone before you attempt a Monster Squat.

My workout week goes as follows:

Monday	Heavy Bench
Tuesday	Speed Legs & Light Back
Wednesday	Off
Thursday	Light Bench & Arms & Shoulders
Friday	Heavy Squats
Saturday & Sunday	Off

You can see by my workout week that I have two days off after squatting heavy. Not only are the two days off from training, but they are off from my job as well. I can relax and use the whole weekend to recover. At the beginning of the week I train my bench heavy, giving me two light training days and one day off before I have to squat heavy again. Also, if I'm still feeling sore on Tuesday, light squat day, I can take that day even lighter, so I will be fully recovered for the following Friday workout.

Diet

What about food? I don't want to get into diet and nutrition, but make sure you are getting enough carbs and protein in your diet to help your muscles recover. I'm not one for protein drinks and power bars, but one of either within 30 minutes after your workout will help your muscles to recover. If you are like me and don't like all the protein supplements, eat more chicken, fish, and red meat. I eat meat at almost every lunch and dinner. As for carbs, I don't pay too much attention to them until I am getting ready for a competition or a heavy squat day. I will "carb load" the day before either. On the way to the gym on a heavy squat day, I will eat a few granola bars in the car. You want to eat some carbs before and after your workouts, to replenish what your muscles used. All this will help your body recover from workout to workout.

Sleep

Do I need to say anything more? Get enough sleep. Your body repairs itself best when you are sleeping. Try to get at least eight to nine hours of sleep every night. For you older lifters, like me, you might want to get a little more. You will be able to tell if you are getting enough or not by how you feel. If you find yourself falling asleep or (what I do in meetings) zoning out so much that you aren't listening and are fighting the urge to sleep, you may not be getting enough. Give your muscles the rest they need. The most important thing about sleep is to get enough the day before a Monster Squat.

Spotters/Training Partners

One of the most overlooked aspects to strength training is your spotters/training partners. Whenever you read about weight training, you never read anything about training partners or spotters. For most of us, our training partners are our spotters. Surround yourself with other lifters, ideally experienced ones. That's not to say that you shouldn't train with inexperienced lifters, but make sure they learn how to spot properly.

The ideal partner should possess the following qualities:

- Strong: If you are going to squat huge amounts of weights, you need spotters that are strong enough to help you in case you get in trouble.

- Focused: Spotters should be attentive when loading the weights and during the lift. You don't want day-dreamers around you when you are attempting a Monster Squat, and you definitely don't want mis-loaded bars.

- Motivated: Partners with the same drive as you are the best. It's always easier to achieve your goal when

Lester (left) and Me in the Team Jax training facility.

Team Jax members have been training together for over ten years.

you have others working with you toward the same goal. Partners that push you and challenge you will help keep you motivated towards your goals.

- Dependable: It's hard to squat heavy if your partners don't show up.

- Positive attitude: Constructive criticism is always a good thing, but a partner with a negative attitude usually supplies negative criticisms which will eat at your confidence and bring down everyone in the gym.

- Honesty: Do you really want to go to a competition and find out that you squat high? When a partner

Team Jax's Training Facility

Having the proper facility and equipment will help make a difference in your quest for a Monster Squat.

Over the years Team Jax has furnished and maintained a small but effective powerlifting gym, located in Lester's back yard.

says your squats are good and they aren't, you will have a false sense of confidence. This confidence may cause you to try a weight you aren't ready for, causing you to miss a lift or injuring yourself.

I think of squatting like going into battle. You want people around you that have your back. Squatting heavy weight is dangerous. Anything can happen during the lift. Have people you can trust around you. When you get under the bar and know that your partners will keep you safe no matter what happens, then you will lose the fear that comes with attempting heavy weights.

Exercises

Squat

Of course, we will start the exercise section with the traditional squat.

The squat is the most important exercise available to you in your quest for your Monster Squat. I don't think we really need to get into all the details on how to perform this exercise, since we discussed it in chapter one.

You will need a squat bar that will be able to handle large loads. There are bars available from the upper $400s, like the Okie Squat Bar, Texas Squat Bar, and Mastadon to mention a few. These bars are made thicker and longer than traditional gym bars and are specifically made to handle 1,000 lbs. or more.

You will also want to invest in 100 lb. plates. When squatting heavy weight and only using 45 lb. plates, the weight stack on each side of the bar extends far out to the ends of the bar and makes the bar bend more, which in turn makes the bar "whippy." When squatting 100 lb. plates, it creates a tight weight stack with added stability. It's nice to see those beasts on the bar.

Box Squat

The benefits of the box squat fall mostly under the category of building proper form, as well as building the explosive strength coming out of the hole. The box squat is performed just like traditional squat, but down to a box.

Find a box wide enough to sit on and strong enough to support your weight. You want the box height to be low enough for you to break parallel when sitting on the box while using your normal squat stance. Rubber mats can be stacked on or under the box to fine tune the height of the box.

Set up in your normal stance with the box placed on the floor 6-12 inches behind you. You don't want the box directly under your body because you will be squatting "back" and not "down." Squat down, pushing your hips back to sit on to the box, almost like you were sitting in a chair. Pause for a second once reaching the box, then blast up off the box back to the standing position. Now this is where I differ from most other lifters—I don't believe that you need to "rock" backwards when pausing on the box. Instead, only touch the box, pause, and come up, keeping your form throughout the lift. Sitting back causes your body to relax for a second, and when box squatting heavy weight this can cause your lower back to bow out of position, losing your arch, and possibly causing injury.

Team Jax's custom made box, has three heights; measuring 11 in. x 13 in. x 15 in.

Now if one of your weaknesses is your blast out of the hole, then you will want to pause the weight. In fact, pause it for a one count, and then blast up off the box, almost as though you were trying to jump. Just remember to stay tight during the pause and don't let your back bow out.

Chain Squats

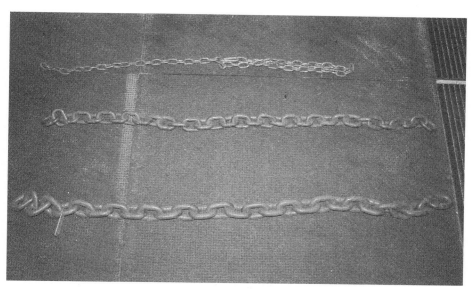

Chain squats are the perfect exercise to help develop top end strength, especially when unracking weight, as well as developing stability muscles. The chains are very unstable and like to move a lot during the lift, causing your stability muscles to work hard to keep you in good form. It works transitional movements. These are the points in the lift when one muscle group takes over for another. The weight is actually lighter at the bottom of the lift when the chains coil up on the floor (de-load), allowing you to get great speed out of the hole. This speed will help you break through any sticking points, usually where your muscle groups transition in and out of action. As you recover the weight the chain weight will re-load back onto the bar.

Here's an example. At the top, the bar weight is 700 lbs., chain weight is 250 lbs., and total weight is 950 lbs. You will have to unrack, stand, and hold 905 lbs. In the hole, bar weight will still be 700 lbs., but chain weight will have 125 lbs. coiled up on the floor, for a total of 825 lbs. In this example, you will have to unrack 950 lbs. but only have to deal with a lighter weight throughout most of the lift.

We have approximately 365 lbs. of chains that we use. The more chains you use, the more of a weight de-load/re-load difference. With the same example, using 365 lbs. of chains puts the top end weight at 1,065 lbs., with around 150 lbs. coiling up on the floor, leaving around 850 lbs. in the hole.

You will need to get chains to perform this exercise. Two smaller linked chain "holders," usually around four to five feet long will hang on the ends of the bar, and be used to hold larger chains. You will also need multiple sets of larger linked chains—"hangers"— around three-feet-long to hang from the holder chains. Hang the holder chains over each end of the bar and clip the two ends together. Hang one of the larger chains through the loop of the holder chain with the ends of the larger chain on the floor.

Get in your squat stance and unrack the weight. Adjust the hanger chains up or down to leave at least one link on each end of the hanger chain still on the floor. If you plan on backing the weight out, you may want two links still on the floor. This will help keep the chains from swinging too much on the way out. With each set, add more hangers to each side until all your hangers have been loaded, and then start adding bar weight. Squat normal and concentrate on blasting the weight up out of the hole. The faster you come up, the faster the chain weight will re-load back onto the bar, but the speed will allow you to handle the weight all the way to completion.

When setting up the chains, make sure there are a few links dragging the floor, this will give stability to the bar and minimize chain swing.

Band Squats

Band squats will help develop the out-of-the-hole blast, but are generally great to build overall brute strength. The bands apply a constant pressure on the bar throughout the entire squat. The pressure is less in the hole and allows you to blast up hard to get good bar speed, but the tension comes on quickly, forcing you to use all of your strength to finish the lift. The tension from the bands keeps the weight stable throughout the squat.

You will need at least one set of bands. Bands come in various lengths and strengths. The ones you want are a set of the medium (usually 2.5 inches wide, and around 3.5 feet long) and a set of heavy (usually 3.5 inches wide and 3.5 feet long). If you have never done band squats, start with the medium first.

Anchor the bands at the bottom of a rack or monolift, and then pull the bands over the ends of the bar. Make sure you and a partner put the bands on the side of the bar at the same time. The bands tend to want to make the bar fly out of the rack when only one band is on the bar. Get under the bar and unrack the bar. You will be able to feel if the bands are pulling with even tension. If not, adjust the tension of the bands where you anchored them until they feel equal.

The bands are anchored by special bars attached to the base of the monolift. (top)

Band savers are used on the bar to keep the weights from hurting the bands (bottom)

When performing a band squat, you will want to bring the bar down a little slower than usual. If you bring it down too fast, the bands will accelerate your descent and it will be hard to turn it back around in the hole. When the medium bands get easy switch to the heavy bands on the next band squat day and when those get easier, be courageous and try it with both sets.

Band-Assisted Squats

Band-assisted squats have the same benefits as chain squats. They are great for upper end strength and unracking power. They are like performing a normal squat with the advantage of getting help in the hole. As you squat down, the tension increases on the bands, giving you more help the deeper you go. Coming out of the hole, you will get a good blast and a lot of speed. As you recover the weight, the tension on the bands is released, causing your muscles to take the full force of the weight. The faster you come up, the quicker the weight gets loaded back onto you so be ready.

You will need a couple of sets of bands, both medium and heavy.

There are two ways to set up the bands. The first is to anchor the bands on the top of the monolift or rack, pull the bar through the bands, and leave the bands hanging straight down.

The second method to attach the bands is to anchor them the same as the first, then load the bar with weight, and pull the free ends of the bands out over the ends of the bar.

My partners and I prefer the first method. We anchor the bands in the middle of the monolift, pull the bar through, then we take some duct tape and wrap it around the bottom of the bands, just above the bar, to hold the bands in place. The other thing we like to do is to adjust the bands so as

Me (1,050 lbs. bar + 1 set blue assisting)

I chose the second method of attaching the bands because I deliberately wanted the weight to be unsteady to work on my walk-out.

to not have any tension at the top. When we unrack the weight, there is no tension from the bands pulling at the bar. The weight we unrack is the total bar weight. You have to unrack and hold the entire bar weight. It's like doing heavy stand-ups, but you are actually going to squat the weight. Only when we squat down do the bands start to help. I always say when doing band-assisted squats, "If you can unrack it, you can squat it."

When using the first method to attach the bands, we use one set of medium and one set of heavy bands for this exercise. The bands apply approximately 235 lbs. of help in the hole and 0 lbs. at the top. This allows us to overload the weight at the top, 15-20% over our max squat weight. Let's say you have a 700 lbs max. With this weight, in the hole you will get 235 lbs. of help, leaving only 465 lbs. for you to deal with. You would have to load the bar to 900 lbs. or more before you have to deal with 700 lbs. in the hole.

When performing the band-assisted squat, the faster you squat, the more the bands will help. Bring the bar down, controlled, but faster than normal. This will help give you a nice rebound effect out of the hole. Also, remember the weight will be at the heaviest at the top, so set up quick and try to break the weight faster. Don't stand too long holding the weight. Break it quick, bring it down fast and in control, and rebound it out of the hole, but be ready to handle the weight on the way up. The faster you come up, the quicker the bands stop helping, and the more you will need to push.

Safety Bar Squats

60 - MONSTER SQUAT

Typical safety squat bar. (top)

Lester demonstrating the way to grip a safety bar. Wide grip (middle pic) and normal (bottom pic)

The Safety Bar is a specially made bar that has a padded harness designed to hold the bar in place on your neck. This is a great exercise to work your lower back. When squatting down, the weight wants to lean you forward, causing your lower back to take the brunt of the force.

I only have a few pointers. You can hold the bar wide, either by the supports around your neck or not at all, hence "safety" in the name. If you hold the bar by the supports around your neck, don't push up on them when squatting. Once the weight gets heavy, it's a natural tendency to push up on the supports, but this is a bad thing. Because of the way the bar is designed, pushing up on the supports will swing the weights out in front of front of your center of gravity, causing you to bend over. Unless you have one super strong lower back, your butt will come up first.

Take a normal stance, set the rack or monolift a little higher due to the padding on the bar, and try to stay as upright as possible throughout the whole squat. Squat down, then drive out of the hole with your head first, trying to keep your back as upright as possible. Remember, with this bar, the more you lean over, the further out in front of you the weight will be, and the harder the lift will become.

Cambered Bar Squats

Cambered bar is a great exercise to develop lower back and torso stability. The design of the cambered bar takes stress off the shoulders and upper back. It also places the weight at a lower center of gravity, making it more stable to squat.

When squatting down, the weight will swing out in front of you, pretty much lining up with your knees. This will work your lower back and torso. You will have to use your lower back to drive the weight out of the hole.

Cambered bar with non-rotating sleeves

To squat with this bar, setup as you would with a normal bar. The only difference is where you will grip the bar. Most cambered bars will allow you to grip them in two places, on the downward bars or next to the weight stacks. Choose whichever works best for you. You will want to squat straight down, keeping your head up. When in the hole, the weight stacks will swing out in front of your center of gravity, so tighten up your torso by pushing your stomach into your belt. Leading with your head, drive your head and shoulders back to start the recovery of the weight.

There are a few things to watch out for when using the cambered bar. If the bar you are using doesn't have rotating sleeves (the part of the bar where the weights are loaded onto) there will be a lot of swaying during the lift, so keep tight and squat slower. Another thing to watch out for is when you hit a sticking point. When you hit a sticking point, you will tend to use your arms to push the weight. Don't push the bar at all, it will push the weight out more in front of your center of gravity than it already is, and you will probably miss the lift. Instead, try to pull back on the bar, getting the weight in a better position for your legs to push it.

Front Squats

I use a front squat harness to take pressure off my shoulders.

Front squats are a great exercise to strengthen your back and torso. Front squats are performed by placing the bar on your front shoulders under your neck. When squatting with the bar in front, you will have to concentrate on standing straight up and down throughout the lift. Your back and trunk will have to work hard to keep you from leaning forward as well, especially in the hole.

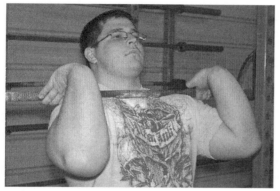

There are a few ways to hold the bar. The easiest is to buy a front squat harness to assist in holding the weight. If you don't get a harness, then you can use one of two ways to hold the weight: the cross-armed grip or a clean grip like Olympic lifters.

Typical way to hold the bar (top)

Olympics style to hold the bar (bottom)

Step up to the bar with the rack height set so that bar lines up with your collar bones. If using the cross-arm grip, step up to the bar and cross your forearms under the bar. Grab the top of the bar with each hand and push your elbows up to create a platform across your front deltoids for the bar. With the clean grip, you want to grab the bar with your fingertips, usually around shoulder-width apart. Push your elbows up under the bar as high as you can and rest the bar on your front deltoids. The bar should be at the bottom of your throat with either grip. Bend at your knees enough to position your body under the bar with your back completely upright. Push your head back and use your legs to unrack the weight. Squat down, concentrating on not leaning forward, break parallel, and stand back up. When you come up out of the hole, be sure that you push your head back and elbows up. If you drive too hard with your legs at first, your butt will come up first and you will most likely lose the weight out in front of you.

Zercher Squats

Zercher squats are a great way to work on leg strength without putting a whole lot of stress on your back. Zerchers are performed by holding the weight in the bend of your arms at the elbows. When performing these squats, the bar will be supported by your arms, and less so by your back. Your back and torso will still be involved, mostly for stability, but most of the work will be accomplished with your legs. These squats will eliminate the compression that occurs on your back when performing traditional squats.

Set up the bar in the rack in a low position, about even with the top of your belt. Position your arms under the bar until the bar is sitting in the crook of your elbows. This will be uncomfortable, the pressure of the weight will be on your arm joints, so don't be embarrassed to wrap a towel around the bar to soften the hold. I find it easier to hold the bar when I hold my hands together with my elbows pushed into my belt. Bend your knees, and step under the bar taking a wide stance. Your elbows will need to travel between your legs, so take a stance that allows this to happen. Using your legs, stand up with the weight. Take note to keep your shoulders back and head up, leaning back a little if possible. The weight will try to pull you forward when holding it like this.

Good Mornings

Good mornings can be performed with a straight bar, demonstrated above, a safety bar or even a cambered bar.

Good mornings are one of the best exercises for the lower back, hamstring, glutes, and hip flexor strength. One of the main reasons to perform this exercise is to build strength in all the right areas that you use to help you recover from a bad squat. When performing good mornings, the straighter you keep your legs, the more the hamstrings and glutes will be worked. Bending a little at your knees will help work your hip flexors. Either way, your lower back will get worked. When blasting weight out of the hole in the traditional squat, the hip flexors provide the thrust needed to move the weight fast.

You want to set up the same way as your traditional squat. Once you are setup, instead of coming straight down with the weight, push your butt back and bend at the hips. Lower the weight as low as you can by bending over, but not so far that the bar rolls up onto your neck. Try to keep your back arched at all times during the movement. When you are low enough, thrust your hips forward to raise the weight back up.

Pull Throughs

Pull Throughs are a great exercise for your glutes, lower back, hips, and hamstrings. These are one of the simplest exercises, but also very effective. You can do them with light bands to stretch or heavy bands to work the muscles, because either way, they are very effective.

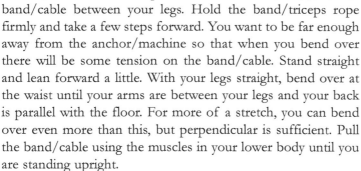

To execute the pull through with a band, anchor the band low around something heavy in the gym like a monolift or rack that is anchored to the floor. If you plan on using a cable machine, set the machine up so the cable is pulling from the lowest position on the machine. With bands, you will just hold onto the bands. With the cable machine, you can use triceps rope hooked to the cable.

To perform a pull through, stand with your back facing the band anchor/machine and pull the band/cable between your legs. Hold the band/triceps rope firmly and take a few steps forward. You want to be far enough away from the anchor/machine so that when you bend over there will be some tension on the band/cable. Stand straight and lean forward a little. With your legs straight, bend over at the waist until your arms are between your legs and your back is parallel with the floor. For more of a stretch, you can bend over even more than this, but perpendicular is sufficient. Pull the band/cable using the muscles in your lower body until you are standing upright.

Depending on what muscles you plan on working, you can take a wider or narrower stance. You can also bend your knees slightly to get more of your legs involved. Play with different variations to see what works best for you.

Reverse Hypers

Reverse Hypers are another great exercise for your glutes, lower back, hips, and hamstrings. They also have huge benefits when it comes to stretching your spine.

These are done with the use of a special machine. There are all kinds of reverse hyper machines on the market, but you will want to find one by Louie Simmons of Westside Barbell. His design is specifically made for powerlifting.

To perform a reverse hyper, lay on the machine with your stomach down. Make sure your hips are off the end of the machine, legs hanging down. Place your feet in the swing arms strap. Push the weight forward with your feet to get a little momentum in the swing arm. When the weight swings back toward your feet, pull your leg up with your hips and lower back until they are parallel with the floor. Lower the weight and let the swing of the weight pull your legs under the machine. This will give you a great stretch. When the momentum slows or stops, pull the weight back up again until your legs are parallel with the floor.

There's not much variation to this exercise other than the weight. Do light sets to stretch, and heavy ones for work.

Leg Extensions & Leg Curls

When it comes to leg extensions and leg curls, there is really no need to do either exercise heavily. When looking to squat big, you want to use both of these as supplemental exercises for rehabilitative purposes. No need to get into the equipment needed or proper form, I'm pretty sure you already know how to do these. The only thing I will suggest is that you keep the reps between 10 and 15 with light-medium weight. One other thing on each: when exerting the force to extend or curl the weight, blast the weight from the starting position to completion, then lower the weight slowly back to the start position. Try to move the weight as fast as possible to get your muscles used to exploding with force.

Leg Press

Leg presses are great to get some core leg strength. Just like the extensions and curls, I'm not going to get into what equipment or form. This exercise is good to throw into a program once in a while, but if you are looking to squat big, then stay with the squats. If you are supposed to squat heavy and don't have the spotters, then do these. If your back is sore and you need to give it a rest, do these. If you feel that your leg strength is your weakness when you squat, do these. And, every once in a while, for no reason, do them because they are great for concentrating on leg muscle strength.

Don't let your back bow out at the bottom. Try to keep your back arched even though you are sitting in a machine, as bowing your back out can cause injury.

Abs

Last, but not least in the list of exercises is abs. Having a strong trunk plays an important part in making a Monster Squat. You will need to be as stable as possible during the squat and strong abs will help with this stability. There are all kinds of exercises you can perform to strengthen your abs. There are a few that are more popular with the powerlifting crowd than most. Those would be: standing up crunches, wide-legged sit-ups, inclined sit-ups, and medicine ball inclined sit-ups.

Standing up crunches can be performed on a cable machine or with a band. When using a cable machine, set the cable up in the high position above your head. Using a triceps rope, stand under the rope, facing away from the machine and pull it down until your hands are touching the top of your shoulders.

Keeping your legs straight, bend over at the waist until your upper body is parallel with the floor, then stand back up straight again. It is pretty much the same way when using a band. Attach the band to the top of a power rack or mono-lift. Standing under the band, hold it with both hands and pull it down to your forehead. Bend over at the waist until your upper body is parallel with the floor, then stand back up straight again.

Wide legged sit-ups are performed much like regular sit-ups but with your legs spread wide. Sit on the floor and place each foot under a bench or other piece of equipment in the gym. You will need to have your legs spread apart, so pick a piece of equipment that allows you to do so. Once your feet are planted, take a 25 lb. or 45 lb. plate and hold it to your chest. Lay flat on the floor with the weight on your chest, then sit-up. With this exercise, you will want to pull your torso up by using your hips and legs. Make sure you keep your abs tight throughout the whole exercise. You should feel these in your lower abs and hip flexors.

To perform medicine ball inclined sit-ups you will need the assistance of a training partner. Set up on an incline sit-up bench with your partner standing in front of you holding the medicine ball. Have your partner throw the ball at your chest. When the ball hits your chest, catch it and lean back until your back hits the bench. Sit back up and through the ball back to your partner. Repeat. To add a twist to this exercise, after catching the ball, hold it out to one side on the way down, twisting your body toward the ball. Alternate twisting to each side on every other rep.

Whether you use these exercise or other abs exercises, you will want to incorporate them into your training program at least twice a week.

Training Programs

Now let's put these exercises to good use. This is where it gets interesting. First, you have to know what specific areas of the squat you need to work the most: speed, strength, or form. This is important to know before planning a squat program. Always remember that your goal is a Monster Squat when planning your lifting program.

There are many ways to put together strength training programs. There are so many theories and opinions that it's hard to know where to start. I will tell you what I did to lead up to my Monster Squat. If you are a beginner, you will first need a solid base to work with. You won't be able to handle the heavy weights

**Me
(1,000 lbs.)**

until you build your strength to a certain level. I have a few programs that will help you with this. Second, I can tell you what I did to accomplish my Monster Squat of 1,105 lbs. @ 249 lbs. body weight. I encourage you to follow my program and become a champion squatter.

Before I suggest any program, I have to give you a disclaimer. When planning a weight lifting program, it is all relative to the individual's strengths, weaknesses, and their capabilities. The programs I am about to suggest will work for you, but the success may vary based on the previously mentioned factors. I will build you a base on which you will create your own Monster Squat.

Building a Base

A solid base has two things: excellent form and awesome strength. Lucky for you, both can be worked with the same program. Now, you probably don't want to hear this, but you will need to follow this program for at least six months, or maybe longer. You need to follow it until your form is near perfect and you have enough strength, using that form, to be able to start your climb to the big weights. You may be super strong with bad form or have excellent form with poor strength, but if you plan on getting under monster weight, you will have to possess the best of both.

5 x 5 Program

One of the best base building programs is the traditional 5 x 5 program. This consists of five sets with five reps. It will require you to slowly increase the training weight. You want to perform regular squats as well as box squats. Most of the other exercises, discussed earlier in this chapter, are used specifically to train weaknesses. Below is a typical 5 x 5 program.

Week 1

Monday	Squats	5 sets x 5 reps	Moderate weight
	Good Mornings	4 sets x 8 reps	Medium weight
Thursday	Pull Throughs	3 sets x 10 reps	
	Box Squats	8 sets x 2 reps	Light day, use 40% of max
	Leg Extensions/Curls	4 sets x 10 reps each	

Week 2

Monday	Squats	5 sets x 5 reps	Week 1 weight + 5 to 10 lbs.
	Leg Press	4 sets x 8 reps	Light weight
Thursday	Pull Throughs	3 sets x 10 reps	
	Box Squats	8 sets x 2 reps	Speed day, use 40% of max
	Leg Extensions/Curls	4 sets x 10 reps each	

Week 3

Monday	Box Squats	5 sets x 5 reps	Moderate weight
	Good Mornings	4 sets x 8 reps	Medium weight
Thursday	Pull Throughs	3 sets x 10 reps	
	Squats	8 sets x 2 reps	Light day, use 40% of max
	Leg Extensions/Curls	4 sets x 10 reps each	

Week 4

Monday	Box Squats	5 sets x 5 reps	Week 3 weight + 5 to 10 lbs.
	Leg Press	4 sets x 8 reps	Medium weight
Thursday	Pull Throughs	3 sets x 10 reps	
	Squats	8 sets x 2 reps	Speed day, use 40% of max
	Leg Extensions/Curls	4 sets X 10 reps each	

Week 5

Monday	Max Squats	Work up to a 1 rep single max	
Thursday	Pull Throughs	3 sets x 10 reps	
	Squats	8 sets x 2 reps	Light day, very light, < 40% max
	Leg Extensions/Curls	4 sets x 10 reps each	

Week 6

Monday	Light Squats	3 sets x 5 reps	Light weight
Thursday	Pull Throughs	3 sets x 10 reps	
	Squats	8 sets x 2 reps	Speed day, use 40% of max
	Leg Extensions/Curls	4 sets x 10 reps each	

As you can see, this is a six-week program, consisting of two exercises in a two-week rotation. The main exercise will be performed for two weeks in a row, and then switched to the second exercise. Each second week with an exercise, you should try and push the weight higher than the previous week. On the fifth week, max out to see where you're at, and rest on the sixth week. On week seven, start all over again and try to push the weights higher than the last time you performed the exercise in the rotation. You need to start with a weight that you can get all five reps for all five sets. If you are unable to do this, then stay with the same weight on the second week.

Notice the light days are the "other" exercise from the heavy day exercise; this is to add change. On light days, you should be more focused on form than on weight, so keep it light. Note the secondary exercises on each heavy day—good mornings and leg presses. These need to be done with moderate weights, nothing too heavy.

This may seem to be a very simple program because it is. I chose the squat and the box squat for this program because they focus on form along with strength. The squat and box squat will have you performing the full range of motion for squatting while you build your strength.

Track your progress each week and try this program for at least three cycles, approximately three months. After three months, you will be ready to move on. Take an inventory of your progress. Have your training partners assess your form. They will help determine your weaknesses and help you plan your next training program. Your form should be more than adequate, and you should

**Lester
(1,000 lbs.)**

have made significant gains before moving on. It may take longer than three months but be persistent and continue constructing your base until you are ready to move on.

Heavy 3s Program

Another base building program is the Heavy 3s program. This program consists of progressive weight sets of three reps each. Go up each set in weight, performing three reps. Keep going up in weight until you have to struggle for those three reps. As you get closer to your three reps max, you can take smaller jumps to get in more sets. A typical heavy day set might look like this:

Squats:

        225 x 3
        275 x 3
        315 x 3
        365 x 3
        405 x 3
        455 x 3
        495 x 3
        505 x 3
        525 x 3

A Heavy 3 program will build your strength. With this program, you will still want to stick to the basic squat and box squat, but add a few more exercises into the two-week rotation to work your weaknesses. A typical program might look like this:

Week 1, Week 2

> Squat

Week 3, Week 4

> Box Squat

Week 5, Week 6

> Band Squat

Week 7, Week 8

> Safety Bar Squat

Each odd-number week, perform as many sets as it takes until you reach your three-rep max for the exercise. Try 50 lb. jumps between sets. If the number of sets falls under eight, lower the jump weight to around 20 lbs. per set. On even-number weeks, you want to try and lift more weight than the previous week. On the tenth week, max out to see where you're at. Rest on the eleventh week. With the Heavy 3s, you don't need to perform a secondary exercise on your heavy squat day. You should push yourself hard to perform the 3s, so you should be too tired for a secondary exercise. Keep your light days for practicing your form during this program, and stick to the basics:

Squats	8 set x 2 reps	Speed day, use 40% of raw max
Leg extensions	4 sets x 10 reps	
Leg Curls	4 sets x 10 reps	

These two programs, 5 x 5 and the Heavy 3s are versatile and will be essential to your present and future training programs. In the future when you find yourself plateauing at a certain weight, you can place one of these routines into your training scheme. They will help you power through plateaus.

Advanced Programs

After you have built a solid base and have your form nailed down, you will be ready to advance. Surprisingly enough, you're not going to be performing traditional squats very often. You will be incorporating specialty exercises and saving the traditional squat for the meet day and for light days.

If you intend to train raw or in gear, then switch the exercise each week to prevent physical accommodation. Below is a twelve-week program with a two-week heavy, one week light rotation working up to a max lift on week twelve:

Heavy Day:

Week 1	Box Squats
Week 2	Band Squats
Week 3	Squats for Reps 5 x 5 light weight
Week 4	Safety Bar Squats
Week 5	Band-Assisted Squats
Week 6	Squats for Reps 5 x 5 light weight
Week 7	Front Squats
Week 8	Cambered Bar Squats
Week 9	Squats for Reps 5 x 5 light weight
Week 10	Chain Squat Squats
Week 11	Squats for Reps 3 x 5 light weight
Week 12	Max Squat

Light Days for all 12 weeks:

Exercise Bike 10 minutes		
Squats	8 set x 2 reps	> 40% max
Leg Extensions	4 sets x 10 reps	
Leg Curls	4 sets x 10 reps	
Calf Raises	3 x 15 reps	

You can see that each week the main exercises change. Make sure you incorporate a few overloading exercises in the rotation. If your goal is to squat a monster weight, you have to be ready to handle heavy loads. Band, band-assisted, and chain squats will prepare you to handle a maximum load.

Light days can be the same every week, use these days to work on your form. I usually follow the light day workout above, occasionally changing the squat weight percentage each week based on how I feel from the heavy day that week, but never going over 40%.

Typical Team Jax Training Program

Our training program at Team Jax is normally a two-week rotation of the same exercise for three exercises, one heavy week with traditional squats, and one down week. The first week we lift raw, the second week we lift raw and briefs. A typical program looks something like this:

> Week 1 Box Squats—Raw to Max Double
>
> Week 2 Box Squats—Raw to Briefs to Max Single
>
> Week 3 Chain Squats—Raw to Max Double
>
> Week 4 Chain Squats—Raw to Briefs to Max Single
>
> Week 5 Band Squats—Raw to Max Double
>
> Week 6 Band Squats—Raw to Briefs to Max Single
>
> Week 7 Squat—Fully Suited to Max Single
>
> Week 8 Squat—Raw Reps 5 reps. x 5 sets Light weight

We stick to this program all year long, except for pre-meet training. The first week with each exercise is done for triples working down to doubles—this is where we get some volume work in. The second week, we work up to heavier weights by adding briefs and go to a single rep max, this is the week for strength building. Week seven is for fully suited squats, to see where we are at in our training. Week eight is our down week. After Week eight, we start all over again with three new exercises. When preparing for a meet or trying to reach a certain goal, we will adjust things to accomplish our specific goal.

My 1,100 lb. Squat Program

When setting my sights on a 1,100+ lb. squat, I changed the Team Jax base program to work specific areas of my squat that I thought needed the most work. The best way to explain my program leading up to my 1,105 lb. squat is to show you my training logs prior to the meet.

Yury (800 lbs.) At the end of 2009, my training partners and I had finished a few year-end meets and decided to get back into training. Our next meet was to be held in March of 2010-the APF Florida State. My goal for the meet was to squat 1,100+ lbs. at a body weight of roughly 250 lbs. Here are my training logs from twelve weeks prior to the meet.

I decided to stick to four exercises for this training cycle: squats, chain squats, band-assisted squats and box squats. You will notice that I train very little while fully suited. I am a strong believer in training raw or in briefs, because I think your back gets stronger by handling heavy weights on a consistent basis.

If you plan on following this program, there are a few things to take note of. First, the numbers I use are based on me being a consistent 1,000 lb. squatter, so if you want to figure out by percentages what weights you should be training with, just take the first two numbers of the weights listed, and that will be the percentage (for example 900=90%, 815=81%). Take the percentages and multiply them with your present max to get your training weights. Your present max isn't your PR Max. If you squatted 1,000 lbs. once but have hit in the 900's consistently, then 900-950 lbs. should be your present max.

One more thing to take note of is the comments after each workout. They will tell you what kind of day I was having and give some insight into how the workout went both physically and mentally for me.

Actual Training Logs

Week 1—Band-Assisted Squats

345 top (110 bottom) x 3

455 top (220 bottom) x 3

545 top (310 bottom) x 3

635 top (400 bottom) x 3

705 top (470 bottom) x 3

745 top (510 bottom) x 3 - Start Briefs

835 top (600 bottom) x 2

905 top (670 bottom) x 1

955 top (720 bottom) x 1

Training notes: Two green and two blue bands were used to assist the squat from the top of the monolift. When standing with the weight, the bands were slack and provided no help. At

Yury (490 lbs. + 360 lbs. chains) the bottom, the bands applied 235 lbs. of force to assist—this made it possible to blast out of the hole, even more than when using bands from the bottom. It also seemed like the help the bands gave broke down faster on the way up, than when you do bands from the bottom and the bands apply more pressure. 235 lbs. is a great amount of weight to be loaded over the two or so feet of vertical movement. The advantage of the bands on the top is that when you unrack the weight, it is the true amount of weight—900 lbs. This will allow you to overload the weight past your max, almost like doing rack holds, but it allows you to squat with it, making it less than your max at the bottom, giving you the speed out of the hole to push through any sticking points back up past your max. Next time we do these, I think we will add more bands to give even more help at the bottom to allow some major overloading.

Week 2—Chain Squats

110 (Bar, 55 chains) x 5

190 (Bar, 135 chains) x 5

270 (Bar, 215 chains) x 5

350 (Bar, 295 chains) x 5

415 (Bar, 360 chains) x 5

505 (145, 360 chains) x 5

615 (255, 360 chains) x 5 - Start Briefs

705 (345, 360 chains) x 3

795 (435, 360 chains) x 3

885 (525, 360 chains) x 3

975 (615, 360 chains) x 2

1,025 (665, 360 chains) x 1

Training notes: Good day. The last few sets were tough. The reps were killers, but we decided to get some volume work, so be it.

Week 3—Squats

145 x 5

235 x 3

435 x 2 - Start Briefs

615 x 1

805 x 1

905 x 1 - Start Suit

Training notes: I decided to treat the workout as a meet day workout, with large jumps and fewer sets. I had to borrow a training partner's suit, since my body weight has gotten up to 250 lbs. over the holidays. His suit fit o.k., except the legs are cut short. This threw me off at the bottom, so I stopped at 905 lbs. before getting hurt. I will try to lose enough weight to get back in my suit for the next meet day workout.

Week 4—Box Squats

145 x 3

255 x 3

345 x 3

435 x 3

525 x 3

615 x 3 - Start Briefs

665 x 3

705 x 3

Training notes: We decided to do box squats for reps, using a lower box than we normally do. I tried to keep the reps at three. I used a pair of single-ply Titan briefs instead of my Ace Pro briefs, so I could get down to the lower box.

Week 5—Band-Assisted Squat

> 255 top (20 bottom) x 3
>
> 335 top (100 bottom) x 3
>
> 395 top (160 bottom) x 3
>
> 455 top (220 bottom) x 3
>
> 535 top (300 bottom) x 3
>
> 635 top (400 bottom) x 3
>
> 725 top (490 bottom) x 3
>
> 835 top (600 bottom) x 1 - Start Briefs
>
> 905 top (670 bottom) x 1
>
> 1,000 top (765 bottom) x 1
>
> 1,050 top (815 bottom) x 1

Rack Pulls Just Below Knees:

> 225 x 3
>
> 315 x 3
>
> 405 x 3
>
> 495 x 3
>
> 585 x 3
>
> 635 x 3

Training notes: Two green and two blue bands for heavy overloading, like week one.

Week 6—Chain Squats

Warm-ups:

145 bar weight and 110 lbs. of chains, adding 40 lbs. per set until total of 360 lbs. chains, and then we added bar weight from there.

Raw Sets: (bar/chain)

> 505 (145, 360 chains)
>
> 595 (235, 360 chains)
>
> 685 (325, 360 chains)
>
> 755 (395, 360 chains)
>
> 795 (435, 360 chains) - Start Briefs
>
> 885 (525, 360 chains)
>
> 995 (635, 360 chains)
>
> 1,125 (765, 360 chains)

Me (765 lbs. bar + 360 lbs. chains)

I often use chain squats to overload the bar with weight above my goal weight.

Rack Pulls (low pin)

> 225 x 3
>
> 315 x 3
>
> 405 x 3
>
> 495 x 3
>
> 585 x 3
>
> 365 x 1

Training notes: I tried out a pair of Titan briefs instead of my usual Metal Ace Pros. They worked out quite well. They gave about the same support and spring from the bottom, as well as allowing me to control the weight a little easier.

Week 7—Squats

Raw:

       145 x 3

       255 x 3

       345 x 3

       455 x 1 - Start Briefs

       545 x 1

       655 x 1

       745 x 1

       865 x 1 - Start Suit

       945 x 1

       1,070 x 1

Training notes: I used a semi-new pair of Titan briefs and Titan Boss suit. All the weight was easy until the suit sets. I wasn't used to the suit so it was hard to get set up correctly. I had also been wearing an Inzer Erector shirt, which wasn't helping. After the 945 lb. set, I took the shirt off and felt a lot better. The 1070 lbs. went fairly well, but I think I should have tightened the straps down for more back support, as halfway up my back bowed forward from the weight. All and all, it was a successful day. I think the next time in the suit will be better.

Week 8—Squats

       Bar x 3

       145 x 3

       235 x 3

       325 x 3

       415 x 3

       415 x 3

       415 x 3

Deadlifts:

       245 x 3

       335 x 3

455 x 1

545 x 1

645 x 1

735 x 1

Training notes: I decided to go light on the squats to get some heavy pulls in. I had problems pulling once briefed and suited up. I tried pulling 645 lbs. and it went badly. Took off the briefs and was able to get in better position and pulled it, and then I pulled 735 lbs. pretty easily.

Week 9—Squats

145 x 3

145 x 3

235 x 3

325 x 1

545 x 1 - Start Briefs

655 x 1

815 x 1 - Start Suit

1,005 x 1

1,105 x 1

Training notes: As you can see with the numbers, the squat went very well. Tried to get on my Ginny Philips canvas suit but it was too small, lucky that a training partner had a Ginny suit that was too large for him, so we swapped. I was using a pair of Titan Boss Briefs. The weight felt easy, but there was not a lot of spring at the bottom from the briefs, much more with the Metal Ace pros. Next time I will try the Ace Pros under the larger Ginny and see what happens.

Week 10—Box Squats

135 x 3

255 x 3

345 x 3

435 x 3

525 x 3

615 x 3 - Start Briefs

685 x 3

755 x 2

Rack Pulls:

225 x 3

315 x 3

405 x 3

495 x 3

585 x 3

675 x 1

Training notes: Good workout. The goal for the month's squats is to push the weight up by 50 lbs. for each exercise, since the last time we did the exercises. Last time my top set was 705 lbs, this week 755 lbs, so far so good. The ultimate goal is to push the meet squat up 50 lbs.

Week 11—Squats

Warm-ups

345 x 3 x 5 sets

Training notes: This is the week before the meet, so things are super light. Just enough to get the blood moving. Now it's time to rest.

Week 12—Meet Day

Squat:

145 x 5

235 x 5

415 x 1 Briefs

665 x 1 Briefs

855 x 1 Suit

1,010 - Opener

1,105 - 2nd Attempt

Pass - 3rd Attempt

Bench:

    235

    Pass

    Pass

Deadlift:

    235

    Pass

    Pass

Total: 1,575

Meet notes: I weighed in at 249.5 lbs. The only reason to do the meet was to get an 1,100 lb. squat on the books and break the American Master's Squat record. I accomplished both on the second lift, so I passed the third and took a token bench and token deadlift. Warm-ups were kept to a minimum number of sets by taking 200 lb. jumps between sets.

Training Cycle Summary

	Exercise	Intensity	Notes
Week 1	Band-Assisted Squats	Heavy	90-95% Squat Max 1 Rep PR
Week 2	Chain Squats	Heavy/Overload	Last attempt should be slightly above Squat Max 1 Rep PR
Week 3	Squats	Medium-Heavy	90-95% Squat Max 1 Rep PR
Week 4	Box Squats	Light-Medium	Keep the sets at 3 reps, this is a down week to get some volume work done
Week 5	Band-Assisted Squat	Heavy/Overload	Last attempt should be well above Squat Max 1 Rep PR, getting close to goal weight
Week 6	Chain Squat	Heavy/Overload	Last attempt should be at or above goal weight

Week 7	Squats	Heavy	By this time you should be able to squat above your PR getting close to your goal weight
Week 8	Squats	Light	Triples with less than 50% of your Squat Max 1 Rep PR
Week 9	Squats	Heavy	Last Attempt should be close to or at your goal weight
Week 10	Box Squats	Light-Medium	Keep the sets at 3 reps, this is a down week to get some volume work done
Week 11	Squats	Super Light	3 sets of 5 with a warm-up weight
Week 12	Monster Squat Day		

When you look at the program, you will notice that I like to perform normal squats when it gets closer to the meet. This allows me to get accustomed to my gear and lets me fine tune my form. I used to do a lot of box squats before a meet, but found myself pausing at the bottom when performing traditional squats, which isn't good. Believe me, you wouldn't want to pause with 1,100 lbs. in the hole.

The other thing you will notice is that I like to use exercises that allow me to squat top-end weights higher than my goal weight. It is my belief that most people miss squat attempts because they aren't used to holding heavy weight. With band-assisted and chain squats, even though a top-end weight of 1,000 lbs. may only be around 800 lbs. at the bottom, it is still 1,000 lbs. that I have to unrack and hold on my back. These exercises also work well with my Controlled Blast squat technique. Because the weight in the hole is so much less, I am able to work on my form and train my body to explode out of the hole with intense speed.

This chronicles the method to my madness. It worked for me, and will work for you also. Just keep this in mind: if you plan on squatting a monster weight, you will have to get yourself ready for it. Make sure you include a few "overloading" workouts in your training cycle. You will be pushing your body hard, so make sure you include a few down weeks for recovery as the meet day approaches.

If you want to squat the
monster weights, the right gear
will speed up your success...

Chapter 3: Lifting Gear

Now, I know that a lot of lifters have fallen back into the "raw" scene and that's great. I have nothing against raw lifting and think that there are some great lifters hitting some great numbers, but if you want to squat the monster weights, the right gear will speed up your success. If you are still dead-set on being a raw lifter, then consider this: with gear, you will be able to train using heavier weight than without it, which in turn will condition your body to handle heavier weight.

Yury (730 lbs.) - Titan Centurion briefs/Metal Ace Pro Suit

There are all kinds of gear to aid in your quest for the Monster Squat. At the time I am writing this book, I have tried almost all of the popular brands of suits and materials, but as you know with this sport, every day there are new advances in gear, so I may have missed a few. I will go over the gear I have used successfully and unsuccessfully, as well as the gear I have seen others use. This will give you a good place to start when choosing your gear.

If you are planning on competing, there is one thing you need to keep in mind when deciding what gear you want to use. You will need to check the gear approval list from the federation you plan on competing in, and make sure the gear you buy is allowed. You don't want to get to a meet, put in a Monster Squat and get disqualified because of using illegal gear!

Squat Suit

Let's start with the most important piece of gear when focusing on a heavy squat—the squat suit. Squat suits come in a variety of materials and plies.

I have had an opportunity to try all types of suits in my lifting career. The ones I will go over are the ones I believe are the most capable suits for a Monster Squat.

Single Ply

Single-ply suits are made of a single layer of material. Almost all single-ply suits are made of some kind of polyester blend material. The ones listed below are all made roughly of the same material.

Titan Super-Centurion	$195
Inzer HardCore	$145
Metal V-Squatter	$165

The Centurion and V-squatter are made of a poly blend material that has very little stretch, it's very thin but strong. The HardCore is made of a little thicker poly material and has a little more stretch than the other suits. All these suits are suited for wide stance squatting, with the Centurion being available for narrow stance. You can also use the HardCore for narrow stance squatting. The V-Squatter is only used for wide stance squatting.

The best techniques for these suits are the Dive-Bomb and the Controlled Blast. There isn't a lot of support from the suits, due to the thickness of the material, so when handling heavy weights you will have to make sure your form is perfect. You need to stay in control of the weight throughout the lift. The suit won't help very much if you make any mistakes. Another thing to note about the single-ply suits is that they tend to "ride-up" on every heavy set, so pull them down in the crotch and legs between each set. This will ensure that the straps will be tight for each attempt.

Multi Ply

Most multi-ply suits are made of two layers of canvas or a polyester blend material, where the poly layers are sewn together. These suits are very heavy and thick and are able to help support a lot of weight. Below are the ones I have had the opportunity to use, and, by what I see at meets, these are the ones that are most capable to aid in a Monster Squat.

Ginny Phillips Canvas	$250 - $295
Inzer Leviathan	$325
Metal Ace Pro	$299
Titan Custom Boss	$499

Lester (950 lbs.) - Metal Ace Pro briefs/Ginny Phillips Canvas suit (top)

Me (905 lbs.) - My single-ply gear preference is Titan Super-Centurion suit with Titan briefs. (right)

Multi-Ply Canvas

The Ginny Phillips and Inzer Leviathan are made out of two layers of heavy canvas. Ginny Phillips suits can be made with two thin layers, two thick layers, or one thick and one thin layer of canvas. The Leviathan is a canvas suit with sides made of a poly blend material. Both suits supply tremendous support when holding heavy weight. The Inzer's poly sides give more spring out of the hole than the Ginny, but the suit loses some of its support as this area breaks down with time. The Ginny provides constant support throughout the life of the suit.

Canvas suits are made specifically for a wide stance. Most are custom made for each lifter, so when ordering one, make sure you take your measurements based on the manufacturer's recommendations. Take precise measurements. Don't fudge the numbers or the suit will not fit properly. The canvas material isn't forgiving and needs to be made exact to your measurements or the suit won't work for you properly.

Here are a few tips when squatting in a canvas suit. It is important to be in the proper position at the start. The thickness of the suit and straps tend to keep your body locked into whatever position you are in when starting the descent and it is virtually impossible with heavy weight to re-adjust during the lift. Another important part of squatting in canvas is to push your butt back into the suit when you start breaking the weight. This will allow the suit to tighten up and the straps to engage in supporting the weight. If done properly, you will be locked into the suit with it supporting most of the weight. It should feel like doing a standing leg press at that point.

One last tip—learn to adjust the straps. The straps on a canvas suit can make or break the lift. If they are too tight, you won't be able to get to parallel. If they are too loose, you won't get the support needed. It's a good idea to mark the straps with a Sharpie permanent marker when you find an adjustment that works well for you. I actually marked my straps with weight numbers at the setting that worked best for the weight. Eventually you won't need to mark your straps. You will be able to feel what adjustment will work best for each weight. As the weights get heavier, you will need to adjust the straps tighter.

Multi-Ply Poly

The Metal Ace Pro is made of laminated layers of poly material. It has some stretch to it, giving good rebound in the hole. The thickness of the material and the design also provide great support. It is built with wide straps, which provide even more support over the shoulders than most other suits. The legs are designed to go to at least mid-thigh, providing a lot of hamstring support. One thing to watch out for with this suit is that it can be deceiving when trying to reach parallel. The suit and straps may feel loose, but when you get close to parallel, it seems that it kicks in and stops you. So try to come down with a little more speed than you would in any other suit. The speed will help get you to parallel, and the benefits of the stretchiness of the suit will kick in and give you some nice rebound.

As for the Titan Custom Boss, it is made out of two layers of a thin poly material. The material is very strong with little stretch. The straps are also made thick, just like the Pro suit. What I found about this suit is that it is the closest thing to the canvas suits that poly has to offer. When squatting in this suit, you want to treat it like you are squatting in canvas. See the tips for squatting in canvas on the previous page.

Briefs

Once you decide on what suit you are going to use, you will want to get a pair of briefs to put under the suit. Briefs are

Yury (670 lbs.) - Titan Centurion briefs

allowed in almost all lifting federations, so take advantage of the extra support and use a pair. The right brief/suit combo can make a huge difference in getting a Monster Squat.

Single-Ply

Titan Centurion Briefs $80

There are all types of single-ply briefs out there, but the only ones that will be able to help with a Monster Squat are the Titan Centurions. They offer the most support of any other single-ply briefs on the market. They are made of one layer of thin, but strong, poly material. They have great stopping power in the hole and provide excellent rebound out of the hole.

Multi-Ply

Metal Ace Pro	$195
Titan Boss Briefs	$175
Inzer Predator	$155

The Metal Ace Pro briefs are made the same as the Ace Pro suit, just a little tighter around the waist and hips. The thing to watch out for with these briefs is that their thickness will cause most suits to fit tighter than normal, making it harder to get to parallel. You may want to consider this when ordering a suit to go over these briefs.

The Titan Custom Boss briefs are like wearing two Titan Centurion pairs at once. They have tremendous stopping power in the hole and are very supportive, despite how thin as they are. These are great briefs to use under a tight suit.

The Inzer Predators are very similar to the Titans: two thin layers of strong poly materials. The Predators are very tight around the hips and waist. They have tremendous stopping power and provide some rebound in the hole. They are thinner than the Ace Pros, but thicker than the Boss briefs.

Brief/Suit Combinations

Here are a few combinations that will help produce a Monster Squat. I ranked them in order of most effective to least effective.

Single-Ply

> #1 Titan Centurion Briefs/Titan Super-Centurion
>
> #2 Titan Centurion Briefs/Inzer HardCore
>
> #3 Titan Centurion Briefs/Metal V-Squatter

Multi-Ply

> #1 Metal Ace Pro/Ginny Phillips Canvas
>
> #2 Metal Ace Pro/ Inzer Leviathan
>
> #3 Inzer Predator/Inzer Leviathan
>
> #4 Titan Custom Boss/Ginny Phillips Canvas
>
> #5 Metal Ace Pro/Metal Ace Pro

My Brief/Suit Experience

So you will have a reference, my personal best raw squat is 705 lbs. at 250 lbs. body weight. You can compare my raw number to my geared numbers and see what an advantage the right gear can give you.

For single ply, I currently use the Titan Super-Centurion, with a pair of Titan Centurion briefs, and the Controlled Blast technique.

My personal meet best for each suit (all with Titan Centurion Briefs):

Titan Super-Centurion	945 lbs. walking out @ 242 lbs. body weight
	1,003 lbs. monolift @ 242 lbs. body weight
Inzer HardCore	624 lbs. walking out @ 197 lbs. body weight
Metal V-Squatter	670 lbs. walking out @ 200 lbs. body weight

For multi ply, I currently use a Ginny Phillips, double thick canvas with Metal Ace Pro briefs, and the Controlled Blast technique. My personal best for each suit (all in a monolift, with Metal Ace Pro briefs):

Ginny Phillips Canvas	1,105 lbs. @ 249 lbs. body weight
Inzer Leviathan	1,050 lbs. @ 250 lbs. body weight

| Metal Ace Pro | 975 lbs. @ 242 lbs. body weight |
| Titan Custom Boss | 1,003 lbs. @ 220 lbs. body weight |

Erector Shirt

An erector shirt is made of a thin poly material and is designed to pull your shoulders back. This helps you to keep your back erect. These are great to use if you have a problem with leaning over under the bar. The only thing I would say about these shirts is to not buy one that is too tight. They are made to compress your body while pulling your shoulders back. They are tight around your waist and chest. If the shirt is too tight, you will have problems taking a big breath once you get under the heavy weight.

| Inzer Erector Shirt | $43 - $55 |

Belt

Do we even need to talk about belts? Most lifters by this time already have their powerlifting belt all sorted out. If not, you would want a belt that is made specifically for powerlifting.

Here is a list of the popular powerlifting belt styles:

Hook and Eye	$67 - $90
Lever 10 mm	$67
Lever 13 mm	$89

There is one thing I will mention that you and most other lifters probably haven't thought about when choosing a belt. Depending on what type of suit you plan on using, if you are going to lift raw, single ply or multi ply, you may want to consider the thickness of the belt. The thicker the belt, the more support you will get, but when combined with a thick suit/brief combo it may prevent you from getting to parallel. I have two belts, both have a lever, one is 10 mm and one is 13 mm in thickness. When I squat raw or in my single-ply gear, I use my 13 mm belt as it gives me the most support. When I am in my multi-ply gear, Ginny canvas/Ace Pro, I use my 10 mm belt. It allows me to get to parallel, and the thickness of the suit/brief combo make up for the lost support of the thicker belt.

Me (1,035 lbs.) - Titan Boss briefs/Titan Custom Boss suit

Shoes

If you ask any lifter what the best shoes for squatting are, they will probably answer "Chuck Taylor's." Before you jump on the Chuck's bandwagon, I have a few alternatives you may want to consider.

Here's a list:

Converse Chuck Taylor	$30+
Vans (skateboard shoes)	$60+
Squat Shoes	$100+

Let's first talk about what you need from a shoe to aid in your quest for a Monster Squat. You will want a shoe that has good ankle support and one that "grips" the floor. Most "squat" shoes (and I mean the ones that are designed for lifters_ have a slight heal to them. This is great if you have strong quads and use your legs to push the weight, but if you want to get your hamstrings and hips (which are stronger) involved, you will want a flat sole. If you have strong quads, then go to Google and search for "Squat Shoes." There are a lot of manufacturers out there, just make sure you buy a high-top pair, as most are designed for Olympic lifters, are mostly low-tops, and don't come with that much ankle support.

Let's get back to the Chucks. Chucks are great. They come in high-tops for ankle support and have a flat bottom, enabling you to grip the floor and engage the hips during the lift. There is only one problem I have experienced and noticed with a lot of lifters using Chucks. Because they are made out of thin canvas, they wear out quickly. Once they begin to wear down, I have noticed that once a lifter gets under heavy weight and starts pushing out hard on these shoes, the lifters heals and (in fact) the whole side of their foot start to push out off the side of the sole. This isn't good. I've seen it where one of my training partner's feet were almost off the sole and the side of the shoe was touching the floor. If you still want to use Chucks, then I suggest spending a little more money and getting a leather pair. The leather will provide even more support and won't break down as easy as the canvas.

I use Vans, which are skateboarding shoes. I bought a pair of leather high-top Vans and used them for 5 years, hitting weights in the 900-1,000 lbs. range over and over. The leather still hasn't worn out. I only needed to buy a new pair because the rubber on the soles finally started to wear out. What I found out about skateboarding shoes is that the soles are designed with a slight concavity to them. It acts like a suction cup. When you push down on them, the soles expand out and grip the floor. These are a little more expensive than Chucks, but they will provide a sturdy foundation and will last longer.

Whether you go with Chucks, Vans, or traditional squat shoes, make sure of two things. Make sure they fit snug and have good ankle support. Most important of all, don't use these shoes for anything else, don't even drive to and from the gym in them. These are for squatting only and should be used only for that purpose. This will make sure the shoes last a long time, and it will break them in specifically for squatting.

Knee Wraps

Knee wraps are mostly a personal preference. Some people like a stiff wrap, while others like a springy wrap. Some like to wrap their knees so tight that they can't feel their feet, some like a snug wrap, and others like it loose. The only thing to say about knee wraps is to make sure you get the proper length for whatever federation you plan on lifting in. Check the federation's rulebook and approved equipment list. Here's a list of wraps that I find to be the best:

Inzer Gripper	$35
Inzer True Black	$25
Inzer Iron Wraps (Red Stripe)	$25

| Titan THP Wraps | $27 |
| APT Convicts Wraps | $28 - $37 |

Lester (840 lbs.) - Metal Ace Pro briefs

Miscellaneous Gear

You picked out a suit and brief combo. You acquired a belt and shoes. Now, there are a few more bits of gear you may want to add to your gym bag to aid you in your Monster Squat. Those are wrist wraps, elbow sleeves, knee sleeves, and a tee-shirt.

Let's start with a tee-shirt. You will want a tight tee shirt, one that doesn't bunch up around your waist and that won't bunch up under your straps when your straps get pulled. This will make it easy for you to feel the fit of your suit.

As for wrist wraps, get a short thin pair. There is no need for long or super-thick wraps, as they aren't being used for support like you need when benching. All they need to do is provide subtle pressure around your wrists to aid in keeping a firm grip on the bar.

When you start squatting heavy weight, you will start to notice the pressure of holding the bar in your elbows. Normally you won't feel the pain until the next day. Get a good pair of elbow sleeves. They don't have to be super tight—just tight enough to give your elbows some support, but not tight enough to cut off any circulation. They will save you a lot of wear and tear.

Now for knees sleeves. Get a good pair that are just tight enough to train and warm-up, with but not so tight that your legs go numb. When training, if you have a good pair of sleeves, you won't need to use your wraps until the heaviest sets.

When to Start in Gear

We've gone over the different gear options available, so I guess you're now wondering when and what gear you should start with.

I'll break it down for you.

- If you are a beginner/novice powerlifter, don't use gear.

- If you are an intermediate/advanced powerlifter, but never used gear before, start with single-ply.

- If you are an intermediate/advanced powerlifting, and use single-ply gear, then it's possible to move up to multi ply.

Beginner powerlifters, I would suggest you stay out of gear until you have a good solid base established. Now, I'm not saying don't use a belt or wraps, just stay out of briefs and a suit. Briefs and a suit will take away the work your support muscles need. When your goal is a Monster Squat, you will need strong stability muscles. They won't get the work they need if you get into gear too soon in your training. Get a good solid base before you start to experiment with the gear. Also, lifting in gear adds a whole new dynamic to your squat. If you are still in the phase where you are learning and perfecting your form, adding gear will make it difficult to do so.

When you are ready to start using briefs and a suit, start out with single-ply briefs and a single-ply suit. Single-ply gear is more forgiving than the multi-ply gear and easier to learn. It's also more affordable. Start by using briefs first for a few workouts. Get them broken in and get used to the feel and the support they provide. After you feel comfortable using the briefs, add the suit to your workouts.

Single-ply lifters who are ready to move up into the multi-ply realm should start with moving up to a multi-ply suit first. Use you single-ply briefs under the multi-ply suit. This will let you break in the suit without having to break in a pair of briefs at the same time. Once you are used to the suit, train in the multi-ply briefs without the suit and break them in. Once you feel comfortable with both the briefs and the suit separately, use them together.

Whether you are starting out in single or moving up to multi-ply, the following tips apply to both:

- Take two or three warm-up sets, then get the briefs on.

- Take one or two more sets in the briefs alone, then suit up. You will want to be fully suited in your workout with a weight that is relatively easy for you to handle. This way, if something doesn't feel right, you will be able to handle the weight without a problem.

- Always pull straps, even if you can't get down to parallel.

- Adjust the monolift or racks up a little so you can get set up under the bar better. With most gear, especially multi-ply, the bar will be sitting higher on your back due to the suit straps.

- Do not compromise your form to accommodate the gear. The gear is there to help, not to inhibit. Stay in form at all times throughout the lift. If you don't break parallel, don't worry. Add more weight and keep going.

Gear Web Sites

Below is a list of sites that provide the best gear on the market. Tell them I sent you.

Ginny's Power Gear:	http://www.ginnyspowergear.com/
Anderson Powerlifting LLC:	http://andersonpowerlifting.com/
MonsterMuscle:	http://monstermuscle.com/
Elitefts:	http://www.elitefts.net/
Inzer Advance Designs:	http://www.inzernet.com/
House of Pain:	http://www.houseofpain.com
APT Pro Lifting Gear:	http://www.prowriststraps.com/
Titan Support Systems, Inc.:	http://www.titansupport.com/

There's nothing people can say
when you get three white lights...

Chapter 4: Competition

Sly (1,000 lbs.)

Squatting a monster weight in training is great, but you really need to get the numbers in the books by doing it in a competition. There's nothing people can say when you get three white lights for your Monster Squat. You put all the effort into training for it, so why not show others what you can do?

Which Federation

If you plan on lifting raw, then pick any federation you like, as most federations allow raw lifters to compete. You will need to check to see what their definition of "raw" is—some allow knee wraps, some only knee sleeves, and some neither, so check the rules before you show up at a meet.

If you plan on lifting in gear, then, depending on the gear you've decided to use, you will have to find a federation that allows it. Check the federation's accepted apparel list to make sure you can use all of the gear you've been training in at the meet.

Once you decide on a federation, the next thing to do is check the record books. Maybe your Monster Squat will break some

kind of record. This will give you even more motivation to make the attempt.   JoJo (770 lbs.)

Another thing to think about is what division and weight class you intend on competing in. Divisions are broken down by age, while weight classes are determined by body weight. Below is a list of the most common divisions and weight classes for almost every federation:

Divisions	
Division	**Age Range**
Open	Any age
Junior	20-25
Teen	13-15
Teen	16-17
Teen	18-19
Submaster	33-39
Master 40-44	40-44
Master 45-49	45-49
Master 50-54	50-54
Master 55-59	55-59
Master 60-64	60-64
Master 65-69	65-69
Master 70-74	70-74
Master 75-79	75-79
Master 80+	

Weight Classes	
Men	**Women**
114 lbs. (52 kg)	97 (42 kg)
123 lbs. (56 kg)	105 (48 kg)
132 lbs. (60 kg)	114 (52 kg)
148 lbs. (67.5 kg)	123 (56 kg)
165 lbs. (75 kg)	132 (60 kg)
181 lbs. (82.5 kg)	148 (67.5 kg)
198 lbs. (90 kg)	165 (75 kg)
220 lbs. (100 kg)	181 (82.5 kg)
242 lbs. (110 kg)	198 (100 kg)
275 lbs. (125 kg)	198 (100 kg)+
308 lbs. (140 kg)	
SHW (140 kg)+	

Me (942 lbs.)

It's pretty simple to figure out what division and weight class you should enter. For the division, just check out the age range, and wherever your age falls, that's the one. Also, anyone, no matter their age, can enter in the Open division. What this all means is that you will be competing against "only" the lifters that are entered in the same division as you. You are permitted to enter more than one division at a meet, but you will most likely have to pay an additional fee. For example: if you are 40 years old, you can enter the Open and the Master 40-44 divisions.

For your weight class, the weights representing each class are the heaviest weight a lifter can weigh to be in that class. The weight of the preceding class plus a pound is the lower weight limit for that class. For example: if you weigh 199 lbs. you will be in the 220 lb. weight class.

Now, pick a meet, send in your entry form, and start training for it.

**Lester
(1,000 lbs.)**

Training for the Meet

If your main goal for the meet is to squat a new max, a monster weight for you, then you will want to change your training program as you get closer to the meet. If you are planning on attempting a weight you have never squatted before, then you will want to include a few overloading exercises into your program about five weeks out from the meet. Your workouts should look something like this:

**Lester
(1,005 lbs.)**

5 Weeks Out   Band-Assisted with top-end weight approx. 100% of your goal weight

4 Weeks Out   Chain Squats with top-end weight approx. 105% of your goal weight

3 Weeks Out	Squats 80-90% of your goal weight
2 Weeks Out	Squats 90-95% of your goal weight
1 Week Out	Squat 3 x 3 50% of 1 rep max

The reason for the overloading exercises are to get yourself accustomed to holding the heavy weight, without having to fully squat it. As for two and three weeks out, you can lower the

JoJo (770 lbs.)

percentages if you aren't feeling it, and save yourself for the meet. Just make sure you take the week before the meet very light. This is just an example program. If you feel you need to work on specific weaknesses, you can always incorporate other exercises into to the program. If you do go with the overload exercises, you will be unracking weights heavier than the weight you plan on attempting, so when you are at the meet and get under the bar for your Monster Squat, you won't feel overwhelmed by the weight and you will be in the best state of mind possible to squat it.

One more thing pertaining to training for a meet—during the five weeks, take larger jumps. Start out by taking your lightest warm up weights for two sets each. Do some reps to get the blood flowing. Take your third warm up weight for a single, and

then take a large jump to your next weight. Continue to take larger jumps up until your workout is complete. This may sound weird, and the first week you try this it may seem heavy between jumps, but believe me, you will get used to it.

Yury (804 lbs.)

The reason behind my madness here is that, on meet day, you will have less warm-up sets, saving a lot of energy for the reps that count, the ones on the platform. At this point in your training, you aren't going to get any stronger than you are already. The hard work is done. The last five weeks out from a meet are meant to condition your mind as well as your body, preparing them for what needs to be done at the meet. So, the more energy you can save during warm-ups, the more you will have to squat the weights that count.

Meet Day

Most meets start around 9:00 am in the morning, so get up around 7:00 am and get some breakfast. Get over to the meet around 8:30 and get yourself a good spot in the warm-up area. Go over to the squat rack/monolift on the meet platform and check it out. Make sure you get your rack height if you didn't at weigh-in, and give it to the meet coordinator. Also, make sure your handler knows it. You should have at least one of your training partners handling you at the meet.

Me (1,003 lbs.) Go back to the warm-up area. There are usually two racks or monolifts in the area for the lifters to use; find the one that is the closest to the one on the meet platform. It is always good to warm-up on the same kind of equipment that is being used on the platform.

Now go over to your bag, lay down in front of it, put your head on it, and rest. There is no need to get up and socialize with all the other lifters, there will be time later, after you hit your Monster Squat.

When the head judge comes over to give the rules briefing, make sure you listen. Sometimes rules change and you want to know what the judges are looking for in the squat.

By this time, the flights should be posted. Find out what flight you are in and where you are in the opening attempt rotation. This will help you to time your warm-ups appropriately. Timing is everything, and you don't want to warm-up too fast or too slowly. If you are in the first flight, go back to your bag, stretch, and start warming up. If you are not in the first flight, go back to your bag and lay back down.

Once the meet starts, have your handler keep an eye on the flight that is before yours so you will know when you need to start getting warmed-up. The key is to conserve energy. A good

thing to do while you are resting is to visualize your successful attempts. Think about what you are trying to accomplish, think about your form, and prepare yourself mentally for the weight.

Me (950 lbs.)

As for your warm-ups, if you took my advice and trained with larger jumps for the previous 5 weeks, you will only have a handful to get through before your opener.

Let's say you are planning on attempting a 1,000 lb. squat at the meet, and you plan on opening with 900 lbs., so your warm-ups should look something like this:

Bar x 5 x 2 sets

145 x 5 x 2 sets

235 x 5 x 2 sets

415 x 1 (briefs)

605 x 1 (suited)

805 x 1 (suited)

When all is said and done, you have only had to squat two heavy weights, and those were suited sets, but you have done enough work to get your body warm and ready for the real weights.

Having only a few warm-up sets will make it easy to time your warm-ups properly. On top of that, if all of a sudden you are being rushed, which happens a lot at meets, you will be ready to handle a large jump to your opener in case you need to skip your last warm-up.

Openers and Attempts

Openers and attempts can be a very tricky thing, especially when trying to reach a goal weight. There's no clear cut formula to calculate what you should do, but I can tell you a few things that will help you with your decisions.

1. You want to open with a weight that is pretty easy for you to handle, a weight that you have hit multiple times in training.

2. Be sure, on your opening attempt, to sink it in the hole, that way the judges get a good sense of what type of squatter you are. You never want to cut your opener high or just at parallel, if the judges give you the attempt, they will be watching you close on your next attempts. If you sink it, they will expect it and relax their judgment a little on your next attempts.

3. See how you feel during warm—ups and ask your handlers for their opinions. If you feel off, don't be afraid to lower your opener-better safe than sorry. If you miss your opener, it may disrupt the rest of your attempts.

4. It's always good to break a personal record, so if possible try to go over your PR on your second attempt. Breaking a PR will give you move confidence.

5. Second jumps should be larger than third jumps. Example for a 1,000+ lb. goal

   Open between 900-920 lbs.

   Second attempt between 960-980 lbs.

   Third attempt between 1,000-1,010 lbs.

Squatting

One last topic on competition, SQUATTING! When squatting in competition you want to try and save your energy between attempts and keep yourself in the proper state of mind. What I mean by this is to not think about what you are

about to do, just do it. Trust yourself: you put all the time in to train for this, your body is warmed up and ready to go. Just have fun and squat.

Lester (903 lbs.)

Here are a few things to think about when it's your flight:

1. Between attempts you want to rest, not walk around and socialize. Find a chair further away from the platform, where you can stretch out and not be crowded.

2. After each attempt, listen to your handlers and the judges. They will see things about your squat that you can't. Also, your handlers will be able to help in your decision for your next attempt.

3. Take your belt off. I see this all the time—lifters leave their belt on between attempts. Even though your belt isn't buckled, it may still impede you from taking deep breaths. The same goes for straps. Pull them down.

4. If you need to re-adjust your suit before each attempt, do it soon after your last attempt, this way you won't be rushing to get it adjusted right before your next attempt. It's a good idea to have your

straps already set and just pulled down by your sides.

5. When wrapping your knees, fold your suit down almost to your waist, this way you can breathe as you wrap. You can also have your handler wrap your knees.

6. When you are called "in the-hole" or "four-out", get a seat as close to the platform as possible, this way you won't have to walk a long distance in your wraps when it's your turn.

7. Once under the bar, don't be afraid to step out if the rack height feels off. As the weight gets heavier, the bar will bend. You may need to lower the height, sometimes after each attempt. The worst thing to do is to hit the rack/monolift after you setup and stand up with the weight.

To achieve a Monster Squat,
it will take a lot of training...

Chapter 5: Beyond the Weights

Chapters 1-3 were more of the "How To Squat" chapters in this book. Even though we may have already touched on some of the topics in this chapter, I think they are important to discuss in more details. They may not have much to do with the actual physical aspects of squatting, but are just as important.

Dedication

To achieve a Monster Squat, it will take a lot of training. This isn't something that will happen overnight. If you are an accomplished lifter, you will already know that it can take years to make even small gains on your squat. Beginners, you will make some quick gains when you first start out, but eventually your numbers will level off and those gains will take longer to come by. Don't get discouraged when your gains start shrinking, just keep training and pushing yourself, you will get there.

Motivation

What motivates you? You probably already have some motivation that's driving you toward a Monster Squat—after all you are reading this book—but it doesn't hurt to have multiple motivations.

One of the best motivations when looking at squatting big is to see what others lifters are doing. Get on the internet and see what others are doing. Go to YouTube and watch squatting videos and learn from them. Think to yourself, "If they can do it, so can I."

Another great motivational tool is to look up squat records. Go to the lifting federations' sites and see what the records are in your weight class, as well as your age division. This will give you a good estimate on what can be achieved with hard work. I will tell you that the lifters holding those records have already figured out what it takes to squat big. This is also a good way to give your goals some perspective.

I can still remember my first squat record and the feeling I got when I first saw my name on Powerlifting USA's top 100 List.

Goals

One of the biggest parts to lifting is setting goals. When you want to squat a monster weight you need to set your goals appropriately. Let's say your max is 600 lbs. You don't want to set a goal to squat 1,000 lbs., that's just too unrealistic. I found it best to set a goal of 100 lbs. per year. It seems that the 100 lb. markers are always the hardest to hit, mostly because of the mental barriers. It is more mental than physical. You have never heard of the 650 lb. club, have you? But I bet you have heard of the 700 lb., 800 lb., 900 lb. and the prestigious 1,000 lb. clubs.

When setting your goals, keep this in mind. Every time you reach your goal and set a new one, you will have to train with heavier weights more often than before. When shooting for a 700 lb. squat, you will be training in the 600's, when shooting for 800 lbs., you will be training more in the 700's. This means that your body will be handling heavier weights more often, so you may need to adjust your training to make sure you have enough recovery time.

Set realistic goals and give yourself enough time to accomplish them.

Confidence

If you aren't confident in yourself, then you might as well stop now. If you want to squat a Monster Squat, you will have to be able to trust yourself and your body, or you will fail. As you progress in your training and start setting and reaching goals, your confidence will grow.

Now there is such a thing as over-confidence. You will want to avoid this at all costs, because being over-confident will make you try things that your body can't accomplish, and you will get hurt.

So the key here is to be confident within your capabilities. In other words, know your limits, but don't be afraid to push yourself to those limits, and maybe even a little beyond. This is something that comes with time and experience. If you train hard you will be able to figure out how far you can push yourself.

Fear

When you build your confidence and establish your limits, there will be only one thing in your way, FEAR. Fear is what stops most lifters from accomplishing their Monster Squat.

If you find yourself counting the weight on the bar (we've all done it) you are scared. If you fidget around under the bar while getting setup, you are scared. If you are thinking too much about the weight and not enough about squatting, you are scared.

Thinking about the weight can be scary. Get over it. You put the work in and it's time to perform. Setup as though it were a warm-up weight, trust your spotters, and squat. It really is that simple.

If you are afraid of the "pain of squatting," be ready for it. What I'm talking about here is the physical pain that occurs during the squat—the pressure your head feels in the hole, the aches and pains we all feel in our back, shoulders, and legs. Anyone who handles heavy weight has one or two specific "pains" that occur every time they handle those weights. You will know what I'm talking about when you get to that level. Tell yourself that the pain will be there and be ready for it. You know it's coming, don't fear it, expect it, and push through it. It's like bracing for a punch that you know is coming.

Not "thinking" about the weight will help you overcome the fear of squatting it. Look at the weight, just get under it, and think about what needs to be done. Think more about your form. Tell yourself "This is what I do. The weight is light." Remember your preparation, then squat.

If you fail, at least you got under the weight and tried. Also, you felt the weight on your back and will be better prepared for it the next time around.

Visualization

Anyone who has been involved in sports has been told by a coach or a training partner to visualize themselves performing their sport. Visualizing yourself squatting will not only help get your mind ready but will help in building your confidence for your Monster Squat. Replay the squat in your mind from setup to recovery.

See yourself setting up, placing your feet, and pushing your shoulders into the bar as you take your grip. Tell yourself everything you know about squatting: the feel of the weight on your shoulders, the tightness in your chest as you take a deep breath before the descent. See yourself bringing down the weight, blasting out of the hole, standing upright, and racking the weight. Replay your form over and over again in your mind—this will carry over to the actual lift. Visualizing it will help you in all aspects of the lift.

One of the best ways to visualize yourself squatting is by watching yourself. Take videos of your training. Watch these videos and see yourself, always taking mental notes of your performance. Watch your biggest squats to reassure yourself that you are capable of a Monster Squat.

Push Yourself to Your Limits

State of Shock

Let me tell you a short story. A buddy of mine was telling me about an intense squat workout where he hit weights he had never done before. He had gone home feeling good, but a little strange. He chalked it up to being tired from training.

That night he woke and his body was shaking, he felt sick—bad enough to actually go to the emergency room. When seen at the ER, the doctor asked him if he had been in an accident. Puzzled, he answered the doctor "no," and asked why he would ask such a thing. The doctor answered, "Your body is in a slight state of shock."

What my buddy didn't realize is that he finally learned to squat! He had been able to push himself to his limits and a little beyond.

Temporary Blindness

Here is another story. One of our younger lifters was making great gains in his squat. He was putting 60+ lbs. on his squat every six months. I was always encouraging him to push harder and I kept telling him that he had not reached his limit if he had never felt light-headed afterward, or never had a bloody nose, or even experienced temporary blindness in the hole during a squat. He would always laugh and say I was crazy.

Well, one training session, performing chain squats, I was pushing him pretty hard. He had already out-squatted his best chain squat and looked strong doing it, so I convinced him to get

My personal record brief only squat (960 lbs.)

another set in and push even harder. By this time, the bar/chain weight was 150+ lbs. over his max squat. A little scared of the weight, he overcame his fear and squatted the weight. This time is was a struggle, but he managed to push through and finish the lift. After racking the weight, he walked over to me and he said "I know what you mean." I congratulated him on a good lift and asked what he was talking about. He told me that half way down the descent, he started to go blind. Coming out of the hole, he couldn't see a thing and when he started to get stuck on the recovery he had enough time to tell himself to push harder, that he could finish the squat. What he finally learned was how to push his body past its limits. He was able to make his body do something that he didn't think he could do just a few minutes earlier.

Catch My Breath

One last story—this one's about me. I remember the first time I got under my monster (1,105 lbs.). It was three weeks out from the meet. I had already done some major overloading exercises in the previous weeks, pushing myself to weights I have never done before. My confidence was up and my body and mind were ready, but I was scared.

I took my warm-ups like I would on a meet day and was finally ready. Wrapping up, I looked over at the bar sitting in the monolift. The weight had the bar bending more than I've ever seen it bend before. It was scary. I thought "How on earth am I going to even unrack that weight?" I then told myself that the worst that could happen is that my spotters would help me with it, so what the hell, let me give it a try.

After my knees were wrapped, my partners helped me up and were getting my suit set. I began to wrap my wrists and started telling myself "You can do this. This is what you do." I was starting to feel more and more confident as the time got closer.

As I got under the bar and started my setup, I just kept telling myself that everything will be fine and I can do it. As I lifted the weight out of the rack and started to feel the full force of my monster on my back. I will tell you this, IT WAS HEAVY! I bet you thought I was going to say it felt light. That weight was so heavy, I actually thought the tendons in my legs were going to snap. Pain started in my legs above both knees and at my hips, but I knew I was ready. I knew this because I was standing with the weight on my back and I wasn't shaking.

The monolift arms were pulled, and I began my descent. I squatted the weight like it was any other weight I've done a thousand times. Sure, it was heavy and I hit a sticking point half way up, but I kept my form, let out a nice yell half way up, and completed the lift.

When it was all over and I stepped back from the mono, it took me a few minutes to catch my breath. It was almost as though I was punched in the stomach and felt the effects. My body then started to shake. If I held my hand up it would be shake like I was on heavy doses of caffeine. After about ten minutes, my body settled down and I started to feel a state of euphoria come over me. I think I actually started to laugh a little. Now, I'm sure there are all kinds of medical explanations for this. Most likely the pressure and stress of the weight caused me to get an adrenaline rush, which in turn helped my body to lift the weight.

Whatever the explanation, it worked.

What a rush!

It has taken me years to get to this point in my lifting, and I'm sure you can get their too.

To squat a Monster Squat, you will need to train your mind to push your body's limits. You will need to overcome your fear and push yourself harder than you thought possible. This isn't an easy thing to do—it will take everything we discussed earlier in this chapter, dedication, motivation, confidence, as well as time. The more you squat, the closer you will be to accomplishing this. It has taken me years to accomplish this.

Once you figure this out, you will be able to do it easier the next time and easier the time after that.

Training Smart

The last topic is probably the simplest and the most important.

TRAIN SMART!

That pretty much says it all, but if you need it broken down, here are a few guidelines:

- When having a bad day, stop.

- When having a good day, push yourself.

- Listen to your partners, they will see things you don't.

- Safety first.

- Get enough recovery, even if it means taking time off.

- Don't lift with your ego.

Like most superstitious athletes,
I like to follow a little ritual
when I know I'm going to
attempt a Monster Squat...

Chapter 6: My Monster

I told you earlier in the book that I was going to tell you the secrets to my success as a Monster Squatter, but I can't really think of any specific secret. All the things you read in the previous chapters are my secrets. Instead, let me walk you through what I do when getting prepared (my ritual) for a Monster Squat.

My monster (1,105 lbs.)

My Ritual

Like most superstitious athletes, I like to follow a little ritual when I know I'm going to attempt a Monster Squat. Alright, here's the situation. Tomorrow is squat day, and my plan is to squat at least 1,000 lbs.

I start the day before. This may seem weird, but I start by looking at old videos of myself squatting, watching videos of myself making a huge squat and even missing some as well. This way I can see what I did right and what I did wrong. Watching myself gives me a great mental boost. I highly recommend you record all your training sessions and competitions.

The next thing I do to prepare is also during the day before. I make sure I don't overexert myself at anything. I want to rest up as much as possible. When I plan to put a huge amount of stress on my body, I need to rest up for it. One last thing for the night before is that I try to get a good night's sleep.

It's squat day. I begin the day by eating something tasty for breakfast, usually with a lot of carbohydrates, something like French toast or pancakes. Depending on what time I plan on squatting, I will try to eat my last meal at least one to two hours before. For me, having a half empty stomach will alleviate any belching that may occur, as well as indigestion. Also, there won't be a lot of blood going to my stomach for digestive purposes.

Once I arrive at the gym, it's first things first—find a spot to lay my stuff down. Then, stretch. I like to stretch for at least twenty minutes. Then, off to warm-ups.

Whether I'm at a competition, or I'm getting ready for a Monster Squat in training, I like to warm-up a little different than usual. On a normal squat day, I warm-up with the bar for five reps, two sets of 235 lbs. for five reps, 325 lbs. for three reps, then take 90 lbs. jumps between sets for the rest of the workout. On a Monster Squat day, I start my warm-ups the same, with the bar and 235, but after the second set of 235, I get on my briefs, whether I'm using single ply or multi-ply gear. The rest of my warm-ups sets are single reps with 180 lbs. jumps. I like to wear my belt for all warm-ups. There is no one to impress by not using it, and it will save my back for the squat that counts. When I'm attempting a squat of 1,000 lbs., by taking large jumps, I will only have 6 sets before the big attempt. I don't like to waste any energy on unneeded sets.

I put my suit on two sets out from the big one. I think two or three sets in a suit are sufficient enough to get the suit on and settled. I never squat in my suit with the straps down—there's no point. I need the straps up to get the suit settled properly.

It's almost time, so I wrap up. When in competition, I like to wrap my knees when the lifter before me is stepping up to the bar for his attempt. I don't use a super tight wrap, so it's easy for me to wrap up fast. I like to start with my left leg then the right. I always wrap my knees from the outside in, meaning I take the wrap and start under my leg, pull it around the outside, up and over the top, and down between my legs. I wrap each leg this way. Like I said, I like a snug wrap; I don't like to step up to the bar with my legs numb. It's hard to feel and control the weight when my legs are numb. Stretching a wrap to its max, when wrapping, leaves very little for the spring in the wrap when needed. One more thing about wrapping is that I like to pull the top of my suit and briefs down so I can breathe while wrapping.

Once my knees are wrapped, I get a partner to help me up. I don't get up by myself; I try to keep my knees straight so my wraps stay in place. Now standing, its strap time. My partners pull my straps to the appropriate tightness. Most of the time, I like to strap up before I wrap, then have my partners pull the straps down so I can wrap, this saves time after I'm wrapped.

The next thing to go on are the wrist wraps. I usually wrap them as I walk to the bar.

Then comes the belt. As I step up to the bar I get my belt on, but I don't buckle it until I am at the bar. As you can see, I like to be wrapped and belted up for the least amount of time before I squat.

It's finally time. I always check my rack height to make sure it's set appropriately. I like to use a close rack width for two reasons. One, when the bar weight gets heavy the bar will bend in the rack so it's easier to judge whether I need to lower the rack or not. Second, when backing out the weight, I want to make sure the weight doesn't hit the racks.

As for setup, I am very particular about my setup. I have a sequence of events that I follow every time whether the weight is heavy or just the bar.. This is a good habit to get into. It prepares me every time I get under the bar. When getting ready for a Monster Squat, my setup is very consistent, with the only variations being the width of my stance. When squatting raw I like to take a narrower stance, but in single ply and multi ply out of a monolift, I take a wide stance. In single ply, backing weight out, I take a medium stance. I feel that the narrow stance when raw helps keep my body parts closer together throughout the lift, giving me more stability. In a monolift with gear, I can spread my legs and utilize the gear more. As for single ply backing out, when I have to walk out heavy weight, I like to step up as fast as possible, but it's hard to get a wide stance with a ton of weight on my back, so I settle for a medium stance instead.

For all three setups, I use a medium bar position on my back with a semi-wide grip. I step up to the bar, spread open my fingers and measure, placing my thumbs just outside the rings. I measure out to where my pinkies touch the bar then, close my hands out to my pinkies, and then I slide them out another inch or so. I use a full grip.

Next, leaning forward, I squat under the bar and push my neck into the bar at the top of my traps. I then push myself up into the bar until I feel it hit the bottoms of my traps. I then rotate my elbows up, out, and back to create a platform across my upper back, shoulders, and arms for the bar to rest on. My contact with the bar starts on one arm across the shoulders, continuing across my upper back, all the way to the other arm. I use elbow sleeves as well as wrist wraps to help my joints with the pressure of holding the heavy weights.

The next sequence of events depends on whether I'm backing the weight out or not. When using the monolift, I take my right foot and place it into position, depending on the type of lifting I plan on doing. For a raw squat, I feel best with a closer stance. For a geared squat, a wide stance is more appropriate. Bending at the knees, I place my left foot into position. Now with my knees bent and my lower back bent forward under the bar, I push my body forward out in front of the bar, enabling me to get my back arched. I then look up and take a deep breath. Keeping my back arched, I again bend my knees and position myself directly under the bar. Squeezing the bar with my hands, I push my shoulders up into the bar again. I then straighten my knees to lift the bar out of the rack. Ready to squat!

As for walking a squat out, I use a higher rack height, because I stand under the bar with both feet together to lift it out. After establishing my grip and bar placement, I take my right foot and place it directly under the bar, almost centered under the bar. I then take my left foot and place it next to my right, but about four inches back from the bar. As I do in the monolift, I push my body forward under the bar and get my back arched. Pushing my head up, I take a deep breath. Now, primarily using my right leg, I lift the weight out of the rack. Once my knees are straight, I wait until the bar weight settles on my back. Shifting most of the weight to my left leg, I take a step back with my right, anywhere from three to four inches. Again, waiting for the bar to settle, I then take a step back with my left, and plant it next to my right, shifting the weight again to the non-moving leg. Once both feet are together, I take a step out with each to establish my stance. Sometimes it's easier to slide my feet out than to step. I like to setup as fast as possible when under the big weight and it's hard to get into a wide stance, so I settle for a medium wide stance. Once my feet are set and the bar stops moving, I take a deep breath and I'm ready to squat.

My technique for any weight over 235 lbs. is the Controlled Blast technique. I like to stay in control of the weight on the way down. I like to think about the lift much like a slingshot. I bring it down slow and after breaking, I blast it out of the hole. My muscles have been trained to fire rapidly in the hole to push the weight back up with speed. On the descent, I focus on keeping the weight in control. I concentrate on all my muscles and try to feel the weight, and I mean "feel the weight," the stress each muscle is taking, making sure that it is being loaded evenly over all the muscles involved.

When I get to the hole, my muscles know when they need to turn the weight around. At this moment I tell myself, UP, and push as hard as I can with my legs and hips to turn the weight around. As the weight comes back up my muscles are trained to know when to kick in, but if there is a problem, sticking point, I tell myself things to recover. A good example is when my butt would come up first. I feel the weight get out in front of me, so I tell myself to stop pushing with my legs and push my head back, this gets the weight back in the proper position, and lets my back catch up with my legs. Then, I tell my legs to continue the lift.

My biggest sticking point is about three-quarters of the way up, right about the time when my hips are done and my legs are supposed to take over. Most sticking points are when one muscle group is transferring the work to another. When this occurs, I tell myself to just straighten my knees. This forces my quads into action and they help me finish the lift. In reality, it is only seconds, but when I am under the stress of a half-ton of weight, believe me, there is all the time in the world to talk to myself.

One other thing that helps me through my sticking points is to let out some air. I find holding my breath throughout the descent is important. It keeps my trunk tight and enables me to use my belt for support. On the recovery, the pressure tends to builds up to an almost-unbearable point, so I let out a small amount of air. A small amount is usually enough. I let out just enough air to get through the sticking point.

Finally, it's over. Time to put the weight down. The bar, especially with the heavy weight, does not stay in the same position on my back. It tends to slide down a little during the squat. When squatting out of a monolift, it's pretty simple. I wait for the arms to be pushed back into position, and then I wait for my back spotter to tell me when to put it down. When I am backing the weight out, the only difference is at the top of the recovery, I will bring my feet together before I attempt to walk back to the rack. I also rely on my spotters to help support and guide the weight back into the rack with me.

I always wait for my spotters to tell me to put it down. If the bar is lower than where it started, I will need the side spotters to lift up on the ends and guide the weight back into the monolift arms. In fact, this is the best practice, try to get your spotters to help with the racking process all the time. You have already finished the hard part. In most competitions, the spotters are allowed to help. It is all for your and their safety. I also like to wait on my back spotter to tell me when I'm in the rack or arms before I put the weight down. One last thing about racking the weight—I like to release the weight slowly and get out from under the bar slowly. Have you ever gotten off a couch too fast and felt like you were going to fall over? The same thing can happen if you come out from the weight too quickly. The pressure of the weight on my neck limits the blood flow to my head throughout the squat, releasing that pressure will cause a nice "head rush" with dizziness and ringing ears. This isn't a good thing when finishing a huge squat. I like to place the weight down, keep my grip on the bar pulling the bar into my neck, then release it slowly to allow the blood flow back into my head at a slow rate as to not cause the "rush."

Top Ten Tips

Before I finish this book, I have a few tips for you:

Tip 1: Don't lift with your ego. No matter how strong you get, there is someone stronger than you and if not, there is always more weight to add. So, if you start to train with a group of powerlifters or even compete, and some of the lighter lifters are squatting more than you, suck it up and keep training. Squatting big doesn't happen overnight, it takes time and dedication.

Tip 2: If it doesn't feel right, it probably isn't. This can be applied in a lot of circumstances. For example, if something feels wrong about your setup, put the bar back and setup again. Another example, you may squat a weight you've done easily before, but it feels like a ton this time. Don't worry about it, we all have bad days, so don't push it. Back off and save it for another day. This leads into the next tip.

Tip 3: Train Smart. Do I even have to go into this? If you don't feel good, back off. On the contrary, if you planned on a lighter day and start feeling great—"in the zone"—take advantage of it and push yourself.

Tip 4: Get into a set routine, ritual, every time you squat. This is mostly for mental purposes, but you also want your body to be so used to your technique that you don't have to think about anything but pushing the weight. Your muscles must learn when they are needed and to fire appropriately.

Tip 5: Don't waste any energy. Don't load your own weights right before you're turn, that's what partners are for. No need to scream and bang your head against the bar or act like a fool when you step up to the bar, this is just a waste of energy that should be used to squat. I'm not against psyching yourself up, but don't overdo it.

Tip 6: "Treat the heavy weight like it's light and the light weight like it's heavy." I'm not sure who said this, but it's a great way to stay mentally prepared for every squat. This goes hand in hand with Tip 4.

Tip 7: Listen to your partners and other accomplished lifters and observe what they do. One of the best ways to learn is by watching others. You will also need to learn to take constructive criticism. Often, others have a better view of your performance than you do and can point out the little things that you never even knew went wrong.

Tip 8: Don't get discouraged. Set your goals and try your best to achieve them, but don't get discouraged if it takes you longer to reach them than you expected. Squatting is a funny thing. Some days, it goes great and others, terribly. Expect the bad days with the good and keep training.

Tip 9: Don't be scared. To squat a monster weight, it will take courage. It will be scary when you see that weight sitting in the rack waiting for you. Remember your training, trust yourself and your partners, and give it a go.

Tip 10: Most important of all: have fun. This may seem like a stupid tip but believe me, when you are having fun, you will be ready mentally to handle any weight.

Well, that's pretty much all I know about squatting. I hope it helps you in your quest for your Monster Squat.

If I missed anything, or like I said in the beginning of the book, you still have any questions, you can email me at teamjaxfl@gmail.com. I will be glad to discuss any questions you may have. Make sure you check out my blog or Twitter for any new training logs and advice.

Blog: http://joeironmannorman.wordpress.com
Twitter: https://twitter.com/#!/MonsterSquat

Now get out there and start squatting!

**Lift Safe. Lift Smart. Lift Big.
Now Go Move Some Metal!**